Beyond the Boundaries of Physical Education

Beyond the Boundaries of Physical Education sets out to celebrate physical education and sport and highlight its potential benefit for individuals, communities and society as a whole. By doing this, it is hoped to encourage the educational establishment to embrace the subject area as a vehicle for the complete development of the individual.

The uses of physical education are examined throughout history to the present day. The author offers an explanation of what is effective teaching and how this is translated into school practice. The evolution from performance pedagogy through critical pedagogy to an eclectic pedagogy is detailed. Further discussion investigates the future possibilities of physical education and sport in schools and how the subject may become linked more closely with personal, social and health education and citizenship. A critical reflection on the current issues affecting physical education concludes the book.

Anthony Laker suggests that the importance of physical education and sport to many areas of social life has been overlooked at best, and misused at worst. He shows how the subject has a vast contribution to make to the personal and social development of individuals and possibly to the well-being of the global community.

Anthony Laker is a Senior Lecturer in Physical Education and Sports Sciences. He has taught in primary and secondary schools, and has been involved in training teachers of both primary and secondary physical education. He has lectured and researched in the UK and USA and is editor of the *Journal of Sport Pedagogy*. His current research interests include holistic development through physical education and sport.

Beyond the Boundaries of Physical Education

Educating Young People for Citizenship and Social Responsibility

Anthony Laker

London and New York

First published 2000 by RoutledgeFalmer
11 New Fetter Lane, London EC4P 4EE

Simultaneously published in the USA and Canada
by RoutledgeFalmer
29 West 35th Street, New York, NY 10001

RoutledgeFalmer is an imprint of the Taylor & Francis Group

© 2000 Anthony Laker

Typeset in 10/12pt Goudy by
Florence Production Ltd, Stoodleigh, Devon
Printed and bound in Great Britain by
TJ International Ltd, Padstow, Cornwall

British Library Cataloguing in Publication Data
A catalogue record for this book is available
from the British Library

Library of Congress Cataloging in Publication Data
Laker, Anthony, 1951–
   Beyond the boundaries of physical education :
educating young people for citizenship and social
responsibility / Anthony Laker.
      p. cm.
   Includes bibliographical references and index.
   ISBN 0–7507–0931–6 (HB) – ISBN 0–7507–0930–8 (PB)
      1. Physical education and training–Social aspects.
   2. Sports–Social aspects. 3. Citizenship–Study and teaching.
   I. Title.

GV342.27.L25 2000   99–053989

ISBN 0–7507–0931–6 (hbk)
ISBN 0–7507–0930–8 (pbk)

Contents

Figures

Acknowledgements

There are a number of people who have influenced my thinking and my work and I would like to recognize this and thank them for their contributions.

Professor Jeff Steffen, now at the University of Wisconsin–LaCrosse, was my doctoral supervisor and facilitated a dialogue that has now continued well past doctoral studies. I was privileged to have worked with Professor D. Allen Phillips at the University of Northern Colorado and thank him for his feedback on earlier drafts of some of the work included here. Professor Jim Stiehl from the same institution was willing to listen to ideas and push forward my thinking into new areas. His notion of global responsibility was one of the catalysts for this book. Thanks also to Professor David Kirk at Loughborough University for his support and constructive comments on my early ideas. The editorial team at Falmer deserve considerable thanks. Anna Clarkson, the senior commissioning editor, had faith in my ability and ideas. Antonia Robertson, copy editor, brought positive suggestions and clarity of thought to my manuscript. And senior production editor, Lynne Maddock, was responsible for overseeing the production process.

I thank my wife, Julia, for allowing me the indulgence to work at the manuscript and for her support and love in helping me sustain the impetus of writing. Lastly, my son Laurie, has amazed me with his unconditional enthusiasm for all physical activity and his absolute joy of sports. He continues to be an inspiration to me in all areas of my life.

Illustration Acknowledgements

Figure 4.1 Redrawn by permission from Anthony Laker, 1996, 'Learning to teach through the physical, as well as of the physical', *British Journal of Physical Education*, 27(4): 18–22.

Figure 4.2, 4.3 and 4.4 Redrawn by permission from Sandra Gibbons and Elizabeth Bressan, 1991, 'The affective domain in physical education: A conceptual clarification and curricular commitment', *Quest*, 43(1): 78–97.

Figure 5.1 Redrawn by permission from Geoffrey A. Meek and Matthew D. Smith, 1998, 'A field study of supervisory intervention of pre-service physical educators via data-based feedback: Feeding back feedback', *Journal of Sport Pedagogy*, 4(1): 43–55.

Figure 5.2 Redrawn by permission from Matthew Smith, Iain Kerr and Geoffrey Meek, 1993, 'Physical education teacher behaviour intervention: Increasing levels of performance and motivational feedback through the utilisation of clinical supervision techniques', *Physical Education Review*, 16(2): 162–172.

Figures 7.1, 7.2 and 7.3 Redrawn by permission from Ken Fox, 1988, 'The child's perspective in physical education. Part 5: The self-esteem complex', *British Journal of Physical Education*, 19(6): 247–252.

1 Introduction

Researchers into physical education, sport in schools and general education point out that 'curriculum theorists within physical education have not been particularly helpful in providing teachers with definitions and conceptual frameworks for thinking in productive ways about the affective dimension in general and affective outcomes in particular.' (Gibbons and Bressan, 1991: 79). This book is an attempt to rectify that deficiency by providing an analytical framework within which to locate these aspects of sport and physical education.

The notion that physical education educates more than just the physical self is not a new one. As we shall see, many sources inform us that physical education has positive outcomes in terms of personal and social development. However, critical pedagogists tell us that the same subject can contribute to a hidden curriculum that allows social injustice, prejudice and inequality. The discussion in this book is not to determine which claim has the most validity, but to illustrate that multiple outcomes, such as physical development, personal and social development and even moral development are possible.

Physical education and sport have an important role to play in constructing our society for the future. The complexity of dealing with non-traditional physical education needs to be recognized and addressed. We will need educators who have a broader knowledge base and a real commitment to producing thoughtful, rational citizens for the new millennium. This new breed will be able, through a philanthropic pedagogy, to empower pupils with the ability to achieve self-fulfilment. More than is available now must be offered in the future or we will be doing our children an injustice. We know that sport and physical education can broaden our experience and illuminate our lives; many readers will possess a deep-seated memory of a moment when they 'stood on the top of their own personal mountain' and grew as a person as a result.

The state of physical education needs a timely examination to place it in the current context of curriculum development, which could involve it in an expansion of its aspirations as a subject. We need to enlarge the knowledge base that contributes to pedagogical decisions about content, delivery and teacher education. It is no longer good enough to say that we know technically how to teach, so nothing more is needed. There is more and I will demonstrate that it is a necessary constituent of a complete education. This is now starting to be recognized, with the government's, and indeed society's, new focus on citizenship and the personal, social and health aspects of a young person's growth within a whole-school approach.

Physical education and school sport have developed beyond the scientific, positivist era of technical development. Post, or possibly anti, positivist critical pedagogists have alerted the profession to detrimental and negative aspects of positivist implementations and have recently begun to suggest changes and amendments that hopefully can produce a more enlightened and equitable subject area. We must now take the next step and deliver the subject area to a level of increased importance in the educational arena. Physical education and sport should no longer be about skill acquisition and performance only. There are higher demands for this subject and construction of a new role for it will take account of its potential to be multi-dimensional, thereby offering a discourse where the desirability for physical education of goals such as social responsibility, moral behaviour and democracy is discussed.

The closing century and the new millennium are a time of some disturbing and menacing cultural misdemeanours. We have a society disturbed by its extreme elements, such as drug taking and violence sometimes bordering on civil breakdown, yet somehow incapable of accepting responsibility for the societal product. Physical education and sport cannot be a panacea but they do offer an opportunity to transfer some desirable social and moral skills to young people.

To understand the forthcoming discussion, it is necessary to have a knowledge of the historical background to the ideas involved. Chapter 2 will trace the development of the idea of multiple outcomes by investigating what sport and physical education have been used for in the past; what importance has been attached to them by earlier societies and communities; and the changes that have occurred through time. It will be established that sport and physical education have had a variety of purposes attributed to them, from preparation of youth for military service, to provision of activity for social control. Chapter 3 will show that there are many constituent parts to physical education. These will be documented and it will be seen that physical education does not involve only the psychomotor: there are cognitive, social and affective elements that warrant consideration. There will be some examination of what we can realistically expect physical education and school sport to achieve.

The establishment of the affective and social domains as part of the subject content is not the entire thrust of this book. It is necessary to look at the extent of these domains: chapter 4 will consider philosophical, sociological, social developmental and cultural aspects of sport and the subject in schools. This will demonstrate the importance of sporting activity and sporting culture as an arena of social life.

To complete the picture of our current knowledge about physical education and the way it is taught in schools, chapter 5 will look at how theory on effective teaching and learning has been translated into school practice. The recent historical concentration on performance pedagogy and the way that this has more recently given way to the interpretation of school practice from a more phenomenological paradigm, will inform the discussion on what really goes on in lessons. Attitudes and perceptions are as much a part of a person's real world as technique and skill, and this point will be proposed as crucial for the future development of the subject.

Future directions are considered in chapter 6. The contribution of physical education and sport to responsibility, to personal, social and moral education and to citizenship is analysed and then recommended for consideration. This potential is proposed as part of a major new initiative for physical education in the new millennium. The expanded role that the subject area can fulfil is complementary to current educational trends and practices and to the political ideal currently being proposed. Instead of politics being accused of hijacking the subject for its own ends, it will be argued that political impetus and momentum are to be commended and grasped willingly.

However, acceptance of political support does not preclude serious questioning of the motives behind some current issues. Chapter 7 debates these issues and considers how much they are to the benefit of children, sport in education and education as a whole, and to what extent they are part of a process of political manoeuvring.

This book sets out to celebrate physical education and sport and, in doing so, to encourage the educational establishment to embrace the subject area as a vehicle for the complete development of the individual. This subject is uniquely placed to be a major contributor to the curriculum for the next century. In addition, the book shows that the benefits of physical activity far outstrip the shallow claims of popular magazines. There are benefits for individuals, communities and society as a whole. This book explores 'beyond the boundaries' of physical education and sport.

2 An Historical Perspective on the Purposes of Physical Education

Physical education and sport have served many purposes in their history and have been used for a variety of reasons. Some of these objectives have been purely altruistic, intended for the sole benefit of the participant. On other occasions there have been ulterior purposes and reasons, serving the cause of the agency of provision and implementation. The use of physical education and sport has at times contributed to the hegemonic nature of society, for example by preparing civilians for military service. The use of sport for social control may seem a little far fetched in modern society, but there are many examples of how physical education and sport may have contributed to attempts at political and social engineering at different times and in different contexts. In this light, perhaps social control has at times been on the agenda.

Health-related fitness, sport education and games for understanding are all curriculum concepts that embrace the idea that physical education offers positive benefits to those who participate in it. In England and Wales we have a multi-activity based subject in the National Curriculum which assumes that there are intrinsic good things that physical education can offer participants, and that school children will benefit from exposure to its many facets.

This chapter will look at the development of the subject in terms of the purposes and motives attached to it, thus placing the use of physical education in an historical context. The approach to such a task will necessarily be selective, in order to illustrate the point that there are differing goals for physical education. This is not a history book – comprehensive accounts of physical education's development can be found elsewhere – but by charting the evolution of physical education to its present day state and status, we can provide a framework which enriches the examination of content, aims, objectives and structures.

It is difficult to accurately locate a precise beginning for physical education because it emerged and evolved in response to changes in society. The English public school system was hugely influential in the development of games and organized physical activities, but this can hardly be seen as a starting point. For instance, during the Renaissance in Europe fencing, archery and riding were among the activities considered important in the humanist education of the ideal citizen. Where did people learn to play the ball games popular on the holy days of the middle ages? For how long had the native North Americans been playing lacrosse? These may not have constituted physical education, but they were certainly physical activity. To go back further in time, the Romans enjoyed brutal spectator events, but their pragmatic nature led them to recognize the benefits that indulging in gymnastics could bring: in the opinion of the Romans, physical activity was necessary for body maintenance. Earlier, the Greeks had a considerably different rationale for physical development and education. They believed in the aesthetic and physical development of the body by means of sport. But different city-states supported physical education for different reasons: e.g. Sparta for military fitness, Athens for holistic education. (This is an early example of the 'of the physical' or 'through the physical' debate.) Many texts which detail the historical development of physical education take the Ancient Greeks to be the starting point. But was there something even earlier?

Very Early Societies

Very early societies would undoubtedly have been more concerned with survival than education. Perhaps 'education for survival' would be a suitable term for the informal, but very important, inculcation of skills and knowledge that enabled early man to live and survive in a hostile environment. What more basic aim for education could there be than the survival and propagation of the species? Imitation of adults by children, and indoctrination into the ways of the culture were probably the main ways in which this informal education occurred (Van Dalen and Bennett, 1971). Conformity with the group norms would have been central to this process. Societies threatened by external influences do not tolerate eccentric individuality. The limited education would therefore have taken the form of imposition of control over the individual for the benefit of the group. The purpose of education was to ensure the survival of the society and this was best served by ensuring that group members were jointly responsible for that survival. I suggested earlier that social control was far fetched as an objective of physical education, or for education in general, but it would appear that just such an objective would have been necessary in very early human social groups.

Having established group perpetuation as a driving force, the content of what education there was is fairly easy to postulate. Much of what constituted education would have been physical; how to hunt, how to dance to please the gods, how to throw, how to run and how to run away!

Van Dalen and Bennett (1971) identify indoctrination and initiation as central features of this system of survival education. As with most societies that have such ceremonies, processes and rites of passage, the aims would have been to make adolescents fully aware of their forthcoming adult roles within the group. Successful completion of this initiation would have had a powerful motivating influence on the youth of the group. The consequences of failure would have been serious, and the younger members of the group could not be allowed to jeopardize group security and survival. Preparation was therefore important and it would have been thorough.

In early human society then, such education as there was, had group survival as its aim, and the means by which this was most likely to be achieved were social control, inculcation of group norms and physical preparation for adulthood.

Ancient Greeks

The philosophical foundation of Ancient Greek thinking on education was the notion of dualism. This was the idea that humans have a spiritual/intellectual manifestation and also a bodily manifestation. The importance of these two components of existence and their relationship to each other dominated much of the thinking of the Greek philosophers. One school of educational thought held the view that the body needed to function adequately in order for the mind to operate effectively. In this view, the cultivation of the body was a means to an end; the end being the ability of the mind to indulge in rational thought and intellectual enquiry. The other view was that, because the human construction was dual in nature i.e. composed of mind and body, it was desirable to develop each element of this dual construction to its full potential. Neither element was predominant over the other, each being of equal importance.

Dualism is further exemplified by the Greek curriculum, which featured two components: gymnastics and academics. Both of the philosophical positions on the importance of the body were catered for in such a curriculum. It is tempting to identify a similarly dualist approach in today's curriculum. The increasing marginalization of some subjects such as physical education, music and art, demonstrates a two-tier curriculum (at least) that privileges some subjects over others. Hence it was entirely possible that the Ancient Greeks held physical education in higher esteem than we do today. However, the place of physical education in a liberal arts education is not totally unrecognized. Many degree programmes in the USA require students to take some physical education courses. Sadly, compulsory physical education in England and Wales ends at 16.

It was a commonly held view amongst Greek philosophers that a healthy body was necessary for the development of the mind. This view was held no matter what the philosophical dualist position. This is not surprising since the Greeks viewed the gods as 'super humans'; a way that ordinary mortals could be more like their gods was for them to develop their physiques.

Because of the fragmented political geography of Ancient Greece, the nature of physical education differed between city-states. A good example of this can be found in the types of education available to the people of Sparta and of Athens (Mechikoff and Estes, 1993). Sparta was a military city-state and the education of its citizens was aimed at providing superb physical specimens for the military establishment. This was education *of* the physical to an extreme. In addition, Spartans were taught discipline and unquestioning obedience. The academic, artistic and philosophic strands of education were poorly represented in this curriculum; physical training was pre-eminent. Athens, on the other hand, placed education in the hands of the family and sought to develop citizens who, although militarily fit, were also liberally educated and well rounded individuals. Athenian education, although clearly concerned with physical development also sought to use the physical to instil acceptable values and attitudes and this necessitated a broad curriculum with no one area more important than the others. The content of physical education was similar in both city-states, with boxing, running, wrestling, javelin, discus and ball games forming a major part of the programme. In both city-states, to be unfit was unacceptable. In Athens to be unfit was a sign of a poor education. In Sparta it would have been viewed as socially irresponsible.

It is interesting to note that Spartan women were to some extent physically educated. However, it was not considered neccessary for the execution of their role for Athenian women to be similarly educated. This is reflected in some of today's diverse cultural values. For example, in Hispanic cultures the physical activity levels of females is not considered to be of much importance, but this contrasts strongly with the emphasis on health and fitness that is apparent in Britain and the USA.

To sum up, physical education in Ancient Greece was an important part of the curriculum. It was designed to develop the body either as an equal partner to the mind, or so that a failing body was not a hindrance to the mind. Either perspective placed importance on physical development. Some city-states used physical education as a means of providing fit youth for military service, whereas others recognized an holistic dimension to education and used physical education to provide better citizens, more able to take their useful place in an educated society. Both interpretations contain strong elements of cultural socialization. This is a theme that will reappear as this examination continues.

In addition to this brief look at the Ancient Greek approach to physical education, it is important to note the contribution made by the Greeks to the notion of sport as festival, the games at Olympia being the most obvious example. The festival, or culminating event is one of the defining characteristics of sport, but physical education tends to lack this. So if the content of physical education is largely sport, then perhaps introduction of the notions of celebration and the festival would make it more real instead of it just being 'pseudo-sport'.

Romans

Sport was always an important part of Roman culture; its place was in some ways very similar to that of sport in some western cultures today. The way the Romans viewed and valued physical education and sport reflected the changes that the Roman empire underwent during its history.

In early Roman times the focus of the empire was on ordered civilization where there was respect for the law; the populace were trained to become useful citizens and soldiers. The ability to fight, withstand hardship and obey authority was paramount. The educational content reflected this military purpose and although there were some activities of a recreational nature, the majority were rehearsals for the business of war. Physical education played its part in this and children were trained to become strong and skilled for the practicalities of fighting or living efficiently. Early Rome was practical, organized, orderly and purposeful, with little of the appreciation of intellectual and philosophical exercise that formed part of Ancient Greek educational motivation. Beauty of movement, athleticisim and aesthetic appreciation were not seen as relevant to the societal machine of Rome. This preparation for service to society in the way that society sees fit is a natural focus of education and it will be seen to have had many parallels, manifested in different ways by different societies.

As Rome became more successful, riches flooded in and the necessity for such efficiency decreased. The Romans resorted to increasingly brutal spectacles, which had the effect of dissipating the respect for morality that had existed in early Roman times. The perceived need for physical education and activity diminished as the populace became more hedonistic. An holistic education and education for citizenship became less important. Benefit to individuals became the driving force and physical education became education for leisure and minimal fitness. People could take the necessary exercise in private baths, but Romans were also fond of various ball games and these were often played before bathing.

The following account describes life in Roman times; it is similar to some segments of our society today:

> Urbanization is causing congestion in the cities to the extent that some wheeled traffic is banned. A gulf is developing between rich and poor. The wealthy have power and privilege, but the poor need state assistance to survive. The rich tend to live outside the towns whereas the poor live in the crowded conditions of the cities. There is an awareness that exercise is necessary for fitness and to counter the excesses of diet. Marvellous facilities are provided, containing courts for ball games, running tracks, pools, steam rooms, restaurants and conference rooms. Some of these 'clubs' are only available to the rich but others charge small fees for the general populace. There are huge stadia that can accommodate over 100,000 spectators. Here the people can watch

highly trained professional athletes compete against each other. One of the games involves an athlete throwing a ball to a team member who is then tackled by the opposition. Another spectacle is horse riding with races and trick riding. Some of the provisions could be called 'trash sport' where men fight each other for the enjoyment of the spectators.

There are many similarities between this account and life today: over-crowding in cities; proliferation of health clubs; sporting spectacles; and the gulf between rich and poor. One of the lessons is that sport should not merely seek to counteract a sedentary lifestyle by maintaining minimal fitness; another is that sport should not be the province only of a highly paid minority of professional sportspersons. Health of the population and education for continuing physical activity are two of the most common claims for physical education today, just as they were in Roman times. Sport is for general consumption as a recreational activity and physical education in schools must encourage this perception.

Dark Ages

After the disintegration of the Roman empire into tiny units of control concerned only with self-preservation, centuries passed before these small societies began to look outward and trade and communicate with each other. Given such conditions it might be assumed that physical education would not have had a high profile during the middle ages. However, ball games, types of football and games with sticks continued to be played by people in their communities. Because of the lack of outside influences, these games developed locally. The more privileged members of society would indulge in hunting and horse racing and watch jousting festivals, the latter obviously being a preparation for battle.

The only unifying factor amongst these disparate social groups was the Catholic church and up to a point the church tolerated such games. In fact, it has been suggested that some games, involving throwing balls back and forth, may have represented the struggle between good and evil; a kind of theological volleyball. Games frequently became unruly, however, and the church and civil authorities then sought to restrict such activities and boisterous behaviour. Mechikoff and Estes (1993) describe a 'morning after' sermon of some severity chastising the peasantry for their sporting and drunken excesses of the day before. Within the church, however, knowl-edge of the philosophies of the Greeks had survived and was a source of theological discussion. The human body was viewed by some scholastic theologians as the earthly manifestation of God and was therefore to be cared for, nurtured and 'trained' as best man could. This would lead to the health and fitness of body and soul. Early Christian monks, on the other hand, believed that the body was impure and used by God to bring disease to man; as such it was to be vilified. Such a belief, symbolized by the monks' life of denial, had a negative effect on the more enlightened philosophical position that respected the body. The earlier theologians had advocated some physical exercise such as walking and ball games. But because of the beliefs of the monks, those educated in monasteries received no physical education. Theology was considered far more important and the study of earthly subjects was ignored.

To sum up, the purpose of physical education changed throughout the course of the middle ages. The legacy of the Greek civilization that valued the body either as a partner to the mind and soul, or as a corporeal guardian of the mind was gradually eroded. The aim of equal development of body and intellect became devalued, and physical education and the religious promotion of physical activity died away. From a physical education point of view, the middle ages in Europe represent a true 'dark age'. While this cannot be considered to have a true parallel today, we might bear it in mind in light of the erosion of physical education, art and music in the primary school curriculum to make way for increased time for literacy and numeracy.

Renaissance

We have a much clearer picture of education and physical education as we come closer to the present day, and more comprehensive documenting of history coincides with the emergence of Europe from the middle ages into the era of cultural rebirth known as the Renaissance.

As the church's control diminished, ideas and intellectual debate resurfaced, with renewed interest in the Greek discussion on the nature of life on earth, as opposed to the church's dogma about preparation for existence in the after life. Increased trade with other communities, travel to eastern civilizations and further exposure to other societies all contributed to the rebirth of interest in classical civilization. This adoption of Greek ideals carried with it the idea that the development and training of the body was important for the production of well-rounded, liberally educated, rational citizens.

Italy was the origin of this liberalization of thought in Europe and the purpose of the new education is best epitomized by the ideas of Petrus Paulus Vergerius and those of the school of La Giocosa founded by Vittorino da Feltre. Vergerius proposed the Spartan ideal of education as a preparation for service, whereas da Feltre adopted the Athenian ideal of physical education as part of an holistic education. Da Feltre's school, founded to teach noblemen's children, was set in meadows on the banks of a river. Pupils were educated in accordance with their inclinations, needs and interests. Instruction in courtly behaviour and social skills were included because the pupils were the sons of noblemen. Physical activity was encouraged on a daily basis and outdoor exercise flourished. In summer there were 'outdoor and adventurous activities' carried out in the woods and forests. These principles of educational philosophy and practice can be seen in many alternative schools nowadays and also in the 'outward bound' movement in Britain and the USA. Da Feltre did not ignore the military arts, as many of his pupils were destined to become military leaders. His contribution to education was the combining of humanist ideals and preparation for military involvement, and also for citizenship, in one package of educational provision.

Although Italy led the way in these new ideas, they eventually spread to northern Europe, mainly through the employment of Italian dance teachers and fencing instructors in some of the royal courts. Physical education was not seen as quite as important as in Italy, however, and the idea of equal concentration on body and mind did not really make the transition to northern Europe. Physical capabilities came to be viewed as means to ends, such as military effectiveness, social skills and gracefulness, rather than as a worthwhile end in their own right.

These almost dualist aims for physical education during the Renaissance era very closely resemble those of the Greeks; as most of the humanist movement and Renaissance philosophy was based on Greek originals, this is not surprising. Physical education was intended to promote the complete development of a person in order to enable them to take a place in polite, cultured society. In addition they would be equipped with necessary military skills, should the need arise to use them.

As well as educating individuals to fulfil their potential, education was offered on the basis of what society deemed to be important. The debate about what was important had already been won by the humanists, and the schools that existed were thus the agencies of society. The liberalization of the Renaissance led educational thought and educational provision: education followed where society wanted it to go.

Native Americans

So far we have concentrated on the progress of physical education in Europe. Obviously, there were developments in other regions of the world. A look at the USA and how physical education evolved there will illustrate the diversity of the subject (Swanson and Spears, 1995).

When European settlers encountered native Americans and their physical activities, they interpreted these in the context of European culture. So what were almost certainly religious and ritual activities were originally thought to be games. Although many groups were pushed westwards by the settlers, a tremendous cultural diversity was retained. In the northwest there were seafaring tribes skilled at sailing and kayaking, while on the plains and plateaux of the centre and the southwest there were seminomadic tribes who relied on agriculture and hunting for survival.

In spite of this diversity, there were similarities in the religious ceremonies and rituals that were carried out by the various groups. Dance played a large part and was used for a variety of purposes, from preparing for hunting to asking for a successful harvest. The activities that Europeans interpreted as games in fact carried great ceremonial significance for the native Americans and probably revolved around the seasons and important times of the year. Lacrosse in particular was played at festival times. Stories and legends surrounding the games tell of the importance of fair play and sportsmanship while playing. Lacrosse survives today and there were other games that have recognizable modern counterparts: a game called shinny was very like modern field hockey and there was an activity that resembled football.

These ritual games and activities were participated in mainly by adults and could not really be called physical education. They usually had a pragmatic purpose such as securing harvests or appeasing the gods of the natural world. In addition, however, there were other activities that trained the participants in the skills of hunting, such as bow and arrow games and spear throwing. In both cases, the physical activities were concerned with survival in much the same way as those of very early societies world wide.

Similarly, the early colonists themselves were too concerned with survival to be bothered about physical education. What education there was tended to be academic and applied. So reading, writing and some mathematics formed the main body of the curriculum. Pioneers demonstrated that activities such as running, lifting, throwing, fishing and hunting were tools of survival just as they were for native Americans.

After the War of Independence, there developed an interest in education for its own sake and eventually, physical education. The ideas of influential educationists were consolidated into school curricula and these included physical activity as an important part. Experimentation with education and the establishment of different types of schools diminished as free education became more widely available. A few schools provided physical education because of its health benefits – sessions in swimming, running and wrestling were offered. Round Hill School in Massachusetts made a great contribution to physical education in the USA by being the first school to include the subject in the curriculum and by integrating it into the programme of individual instruction for every pupil. What we read today about the importance that Round Hill placed on physical development is similar to what we know about da Feltre's school in Renaissance Italy: the subject was taught because it developed a healthy body and promoted an active mind.

In about a hundred years, physical education in the USA had changed from being concerned exclusively with survival, to being included in school curricula because of its important contribution to individual personal development.

Public Schools

In the early to mid-nineteenth century the well known boys' independent schools, known as English public schools, were founded. They were a mixture of denominational, proprietary and headmaster-owned schools.

But whatever their origins, all developed a strong tradition of games playing and athletic achievement, known as 'athleticism' (Mangan, 1981). This was a strongly dominant ideology from the mid-nineteenth century until the Second World War. From about 1850 games were included as an integral part of the school curriculum; pupils and to some extent staff too were expected to become involved. As Mangan points out, it is a commonly held misconception that Thomas Arnold at Rugby was largely responsible for the elevation of the school games system. In fact it was mainly later headmasters of other schools who saw the moral, social and cultural possibilities of team games.

Pupils at these schools had been left to their own devices for much of their leisure time. A few played informal games of sorts, but the main pursuit was roaming the local countryside hunting small animals and birds. When G.E.L. Cotton arrived as head at Marlborough in 1851 from Rugby he began to introduce games as a formal part of the curriculum. The games were used largely as a means of social control, to keep pupils away from the illegal pursuits of poaching and trespass to which they had become prone. Although pursuing the education of the privileged these sons of clergy and aristocracy were so unruly that they had to be subjected to elements of social control in the guise of sporting participation. It is somewhat ironic that those who were later to be associated with the implementation of education and the process of social control were themselves subject to a controlling influence through sports on the playing field.

Summary

This brief survey of some of the history of physical education was made to show how physical education can be used to achieve different outcomes. These have invariably been linked very closely with the demands and needs of society at the time. We have seen that from earliest times education was used as a means of social control through the establishment of group norms and that physical education was used for group survival and preparation for adulthood.

The Greeks used physical education either to develop the body as an equal partner to the mind, or so that a failing body was not a hindrance to the mind. In some city-states fit youths were needed for military service, while other city-states recognized an holistic purpose for education, using physical education to provide citizens better able to take a useful place in society. The dichotomy between education *of* the physical, using physical education for a single purpose, and education *through* the physical, making use of multiple outcomes, was illustrated by the different educational philosophies of Sparta and Athens. This dichotomy continues today.

The way that the Romans used physical education has many parallels today. Initially used to provide soldiers for war, its purpose eventually became that of minimal fitness maintenance and education for leisure. Concerns such as health of the population and continuing physical activity are two items high on the physical education agenda today.

The reversion to Greek ideals during the Renaissance identified the development of the complete person as a priority, and that encompassed physical development. Such fully educated people were needed to be able to take their place in a polite, cultured society. As a component of a complete education, physical education was serving the needs of society.

We have so far seen that physical education has been used for the purposes of survival, social control, military fitness, health, holistic development and citizen education. This constitutes quite an impressive accomplishment for a subject that many marginalize as just 'playing games'. Many of the benefits to individuals and to society in general are completely open and acknowledged. But a critical analyst might well suggest ulterior and hidden motives for including physical education as a component of education. This idea, of an ulterior and hidden curriculum, will be explored later.

To bring this examination into the present, we must now look at what constitute the aims, objectives and purposes of physical education in contemporary times.

3 Contemporary Physical Education
Aims, Objectives and Purposes

From the name, physical education, one might expect the school subject to consist of education of the physical, through the physical and about the physical. Unfortunately characterization of the subject is not so easy and there are many aspects that need to be considered before a definitive statement can be made about what constitute the aims and objectives of physical education. This is not intended as a meta-analysis of research into physical education teaching and learning, but is an attempt to describe and then synthesize into a digestible package what we know.

When the aims are stated, the physical are generally in the minority. In a survey of sixteen teachers, Underwood (1983) found that the top five aims mentioned for physical education were skill acquisition; education for leisure; health and fitness; socialization; and enjoyment. Only two of these are physical, the other three are affective, social or cognitive.

A broader view is taken by Willgoose (1984) whose statements of aims and purposes has a theoretical rather than experimental basis. Willgoose states that the major objectives are to develop and maintain physical fitness and motor skills, social competency and intellectual competency. We see that the physical accounts for half the outcomes. (Willgoose also discusses whether physical education is in fact the correct name for the subject when so few outcomes appear to be physical: he discusses the merits of subject titles such as human movement, movement education, kinesiology and sports education.)

Jewett (1978) lists twenty-two purposes, categorized under three concepts. 'Man, Master of Himself' includes what is nessecary for man to fulfil his 'human development potential'. Physical items within this concept are listed alongside affective, or somatopsychic, items. (This somatopsychic aspect of physical education is also discussed and in much greater depth by Harris (1973), who claims a range of non-physical benefits for physical activity.) Jewett's second concept is almost purely physical and is entitled 'Man in Space' – where space refers to the physical environment. This involves man's movement in the environment and his physical and spatial relationships to objects, other persons and himself. The last concept is that of 'Man in a Social World' and, as its name suggests, it is concerned with cooperation, motivation, group goals and the strengthening of cultural heritage, all leading to adequate socialization. (It should be noted that the gendered language that Jewett uses in her analysis is used in the generic sense.) The three concepts have outcomes that may be achieved by the physical activity of the pupils, but the outcomes themselves may not necessarily be physical.

This idea of multiple outcomes is supported by many authorities. Martens (1975) claims that physical education's functions are first, the teaching of skills and knowledge about fitness and movement and second, the teaching of interpersonal relationships.

The Physically Educated Person

To expand the proposition that physical education's purposes are partially non-physical, the National Association for Sport and Physical Education (NASPE), in the USA, describes a physically educated person in its *Outcomes* project (1992). Such a person will have skills necessary to perform a variety of physical activities; be physically fit; participate regularly in physical activity; know the implications and the benefits of involvement in physical activities; and value physical activity and its contributions to a healthy lifestyle. Of this five-part definition, two parts are obviously non-physical. Within the five headings are twenty specific outcomes, nine of which are physical and eleven of which are non-physical. In conjunction with this definition of a physically educated person, NASPE has produced a series of benchmarks for children in schools at various grades or levels. In general terms the affective and cognitive benchmarks form a greater proportion of the total as the pupil progresses through school. A later document from NASPE (1995) expands the notion of the physically educated student (as opposed to person) into one who demonstrates competency in many activities, applies movement concepts to learn new skills, has a physically active lifestyle, is physically fit, demonstrates responsible personal and social behaviour, understands and respects differences in people, and understands the social and affective aspects of physical activity. Again, it can be seen that the last three characteristics are non-physical in nature. In addition, NASPE states that by the 8th grade (13 years old) children should begin to recognize the role of physical activity in society.

Some time ago the Department of Education and Science (1977: 80) elaborated on Martens' second function of physical education – interpersonal relationships:

> PE's contribution to the social and ethical aspects of personal development can be considerable, involving as it does co-operation and competition. Games, with their codes of rules, give experience of actions within structured situations, and of personal reaction and

initiative within an accepted framework. The general human need to participate in various activities is as much concerned with the patterning of relationships as with the expenditure of physical energy. Acceptable social behaviour and social responsibility are encouraged and developed by means of these latter experiences.

Although this has since been superseded by the National Curriculum, which will be discussed later, it is clear that, at that time, the highest educational authority in Britain was claiming a socialization and social control process for physical education. Physical education was seen as a vehicle for achieving socially desirable traits in young adults.

Armstrong and Biddle (1992) criticize the idea that non-physical outcomes can be claimed for physical education. It is assumed that participation in particular activities produces positive changes in the individual's moral behaviour and personality. Armstrong and Biddle claim that there is little scienitific evidence that supports this assumption. They do however, go on to say that there is little doubt that positive changes can be brought about by professional, skilful leadership in most activities. Additionally, a meta-analysis by Gruber (1986) found evidence of a positive influence of physical activity on self-esteem.

National Curriculum Physical Education

Physical education is one of the core subjects of the current National Curriculum (Department for Education, 1995) and is compulsory in every year of compulsory schooling. The content of the subject changes at each age group or Key Stage, but there is a set of general requirements for the subject that remains the same throughout. Although there are no aims mentioned in the statutory National Curriculum of 1992 (Department of Education and Science, 1992), the non-statutory guidance included in this document lists aims such as physical competency and development; knowing and valuing the benefits of physical activity; and appreciating skilful and creative performance. The 1992 curriculum also suggested that physical education could contribute to the development of problem solving skills, the establishment of self-esteem, and the development of interpersonal skills. Pupils were also expected to develop commitment, fairness and enthusiasm. The requirements of the 1995 revision to the National Curriculum say first that physical education must promote physical activity. This includes being active; adopting good posture and appropriate use of the body; engaging in activities that develop cardiovascular health, flexibility, strength and endurance; and maintaining good personal hygiene. Second, physical education is required to develop positive attitudes. This includes the conventions of fair play and competition; sporting behaviour as individuals, team members and spectators; coping with success and failure; trying hard; and being mindful of others and the environment. Last, physical education must teach pupils to ensure safe practice by responding to instructions; following rules, etiquettes and codes for different activities; knowing about safety and clothing, footwear and jewellery; knowing how to lift and carry; and knowing how to warm up and recover from exercise. This is an extensive brief for physical education in relation to the pupils who are taught it, and these requirements permeate all levels of the school subject curriculum. Within each of the Key Stages what is expected of the pupils is different and reflects a spread of physical, cognitive and affective outcomes.

On both sides of the Atlantic then, the national authorities and individual experts are in agreement that the subject of physical education has much to offer in the affective, social and cognitive areas, in addition to supporting and aiding the physical development of pupils; in some cases the social and affective areas are claimed to be far in excess of the physical.

A contradiction occurs, however, when we compare what the authorities say should be taught and what is actually taught in schools. Siedentop (1976, 1991) claims that it is only the activities done in physical education that form the content of physical education. The contradiction lies in the fact that the content is generally completely physical but it is suggested that pupils learn many non-physical characteristics from it. This mismatch between what is taught and what is expected to be learned will be discussed later.

Physical Education Curriculum Domains

From the discussion on the aims, objectives and purposes that are claimed and expected for physical education, it can be seen that these aims can be categorized into groups that share similar properties. These groups are called the domains of physical education. What are these domains and how were they arrived at?

Based on a review of selected literature Kirk (1993) identified three domains of physical education: psychomotor, affective and cognitive. These categorize the curriculum at the time the selected literature was written. However, in response to Siedentop (1991), Tousignant and Siedentop (1983), and Tinning and Siedentop (1985), who all comment on a student social agenda in lessons, Kirk added a fourth domain, 'social' to the list. This addition is supported by various authors and authoritative bodies, as described below.

Crum (1985) developed a questionnaire that asked pupils to comment on what they had learned in physical education. The twenty-four items on the Likert-type scale were categorized into technomotor, sociomotor, cognitive–reflective and affective. These four domains exactly match those of Kirk: the technomotor being the psychomotor or physical; the sociomotor being the social; the cognitive; and the affective. This categorization of the areas of the physical education curriculum is thus supported by the literature and has proved effective in researching what pupils think of the subject.

Additional support is given to this categorization by the NASPE *Outcomes* project (1992). The twenty attributes of a physically educated person fall easily into the four domains. First, those attributes that are broadly described as 'having skills', 'being fit' and 'participating regularly' relate to the physical domain. Second, knowing the benefits of involvement in physical activity relates to the cognitive domain. And third, valuing physical activity relates to the affective domain and also to the social domain.

A survey carried out in schools in England and Wales (Physical Education Association of Great Britain and Northern Ireland, 1987) found that the top nine teaching objectives of secondary physical education teachers were (not in order) motor skills, physical development and leisure (physical domain); cognitive development and aesthetic appreciation (cognitive domain); social competence (social domain); self-realization, moral development and emotional stability (affective domain).

The aims, objectives and purposes of physical education can be assigned to the domains of the subject, thus validating them as a viable framework for critically analysing the subject.

If we assign the aims already discussed to the domains of physical education, we describe what NASPE would call a 'physically educated person'. It must be remembered that this 'physically educated person' is an ideal created by the sources consulted. It is only one view, albeit a common one supported by a breadth of literature, documentation and authoritative bodies. So how would we describe such a person?

They would be physically competent, engaging regularly in appropriate physical activities, healthy and hygienic, fit, supple, strong, and skilful in a variety of activities. They would know how to use their leisure time wisely, be intellectually competent, know how to become and stay fit and recognize the benefits of exercise. They would also know about the rules and codes of conduct associated with various sports, how to be safe when playing those sports and would be good at problem solving. They would have good social skills and interpersonal relationships, manifested as good social behaviour and social responsibility; in short, they would be socially competent. They would be motivated, cooperative towards group goals, value physical activity and be ethical. They would appreciate skilful and creative performance, have good self-esteem, and be fair and enthusiastic. They could cope with success and failure, be sporting and competitive, care about others and the environment and have positive attitudes towards physical activity.

The characteristics of this 'physically educated person' are all considered to be good. This is the type of person that is socially acceptable and has been correctly socialized and groomed in the dominant culture to take a useful place in society. They would not be a burden on, or challenging of, society. In fact, such a person would be too good to be true! (Maybe that is why sportsmen are more interesting when they have flaws: while team captains and head boys and girls tend to conform to the type of 'physically educated persons', the stars, characters and geniuses of sport are always slightly set apart from the norm.)

All this is claimed for physical education, but that does not mean that it is achieved. We need to look at the evidence to determine whether physical education really does all that is claimed for it.

Does Physical Education Really Do It All?

Physical

The National Curriculum states that the greatest emphasis in physical education should be placed on the actual performance aspect of the subject. Teachers should mainly teach physical skills; the concentration should be on education *of* the physical. The end-of-Key-Stage descriptions that are part of the National Curriculum in physical education tell us what pupils are expected to be able to do at certain levels.

At the end of Key Stage 1 (5 to 7 years) pupils are expected to 'plan and perform simple skills safely, and show control in linking actions together. They improve their performance through practising their skills'. At Key Stage 2 (7 to 11 years) they are expected to have developed so that they can 'practise, improve and refine performance, and repeat a series of movements they have performed previously, with increasing control and accuracy . . . They sustain energetic activity over appropriate periods of time'.

The end of this Key Stage marks the end of primary education, with the pupils now progressing to secondary school. By the end of Key Stage 3 (11 to 14 years) pupils should be able to 'plan or compose more complex sequences of movements. They adapt and refine existing skills and apply these to new situations. Pupils show that they can use skills with precision, and perform sequences with greater clarity and fluency. . . . [They] demonstrate how to prepare for particular activities and how to recover after vigorous physical activity.' And finally there is Key Stage 4 (14 to 16 years) which takes pupils to the end of compulsory schooling; 'Pupils demonstrate increasingly refined techniques in their selected activities. Their performance is more consistent and effective. They anticipate responses from others and use this information to adapt their own performance. . . . They regularly participate in health-promoting physical activity' (Department for Education, 1995).

The ways in which teachers can improve skills are well known. Research in the mid-1970s in the USA clearly identified certain teacher behaviours that were crucial in aiding skill learning. Feedback on performance, motivation, and the ability to identify and correct group and individual errors were found to be the main teacher behaviours that encouraged skill learning. Much of this research was carried out using systematic observation techniques that recorded and coded teacher behaviours. Smith,

Kerr and Wang (1993) conducted some research using experienced teachers in English schools. They found that the teachers spent relatively large amounts of time in the behaviours that promoted physical skill learning. This meant that these teachers were quite active during periods of pupil practice and spent little time passively monitoring the pupils. Laker (1995a) investigated teaching behaviour in a sample of student teachers. Although not as experienced as the sample of in-service teachers, the student teachers demonstrated effective teaching behaviours, which in turn encouraged pupil skill learning.

The assessment of physical ability and skill level should not be problematic. The performance is on display, it is in the public domain. Some areas, such as timed performances and distances in athletics and swimming lend themselves to objective measurement. Game play and games skill performance are also visible, but the assessment can be more subjective. However, there are instruments to measure such activities if required (Oslin, Mitchell and Griffin, 1998). Most problematic is the assessment of the aesthetic areas of the curriculum such as gymnastics and dance. Nevertheless, Carroll (1994) clearly shows that this can be done effectively by means of collection of evidence against set criteria, and moderation.

It seems, then, that the teaching of the physical aspects of the National Curriculum subject is being fairly well done. Teachers are required to concentrate on the physical aspects, to assess and report on these aspects and the evidence suggests that this is in fact what happens.

Cognitive

If we again look at the end-of-Key-Stage descriptions from the National Curriculum, we can make a judgement about whether physical education can achieve what it claims. Key Stage 1 pupils are expected to be able to talk about practical performances and make simple judgements. They should also be able to describe changes to the body during exercise. The main difference at Key Stage 2 is that pupils are expected to understand what happens to their body during exercise. They should also use the judgements they make to improve performances. In real terms very few cognitive skills and abilities are expected of primary school pupils. With such low expectations it is not surprising that the cognitive element is easily achieved.

At the secondary level, Key Stage 3 pupils should know various rules and how to apply them. They should also know the short-term and long-term effects of exercise on the body. At Key Stage 4, school children are expected to undertake different roles, such as coach and official.

These knowledges are arranged sequentially and appear to present an increasingly relevant preparation for participation, spectatorship, coaching and so on, but there is very little real content, especially when compared to what is claimed in the general requirements for the subject. It could be argued that the cognitive element of physical education is covered by the public examinations of GCSE and CSE A level and this may well be the case. But examination physical education is not the same as curriculum physical education, although at Key Stage 4 and beyond it is quite likely that the two will be combined.

The traditional methods of assessing knowledge, i.e. written and oral tests, are not particularly appropriate for curriculum physical education. Nevertheless, teachers have to assess and report on their pupils' progress in this field. This is usually accomplished by deciding how pupils apply the knowledge in practical situations. The majority of examinations in physical education and sports studies test theoretical knowledge, although GCSE and A-level physical education do have practical elements. As Carroll (1994) confirms, physical education has a large cognitive element and function and this is assessed sometimes in traditionally public examinations and sometimes practically, in curriculum time. The introduction of examinations and a cognitive component into what was previously a purely practical and recreational subject has given some form of academic legitimation to school physical education, often a marginal subject in the past. Teachers and others in the profession have keenly embraced these cognitive elements, not only because they value that particular knowledge, but also because they value that particular *type* of knowledge and the effect it could have on the credibility of the profession: along with the practical components, it is seen as valuable, it can be taught and it can be assessed.

Affective

The 'physically educated person' shows many affective characteristics. Positive attitudes towards physical activity, good self-esteem, a commitment to fair play and an appreciation of skilful and creative performance are only a few of these characteristics.

The end-of-Key-Stage descriptions from the National Curriculum hardly mention the affective domain at all, Key Stage 1 merely suggesting that pupils should be able to work with a partner. This is unfortunate because there is some evidence that suggests that even kindergarten pupils can improve prosocial behaviours (Grineski, 1989). When comparing groups that were taught cooperative games and competitive games, the group taught cooperative games showed a much higher incidence of cooperative behaviour (see p. 42). This shows that the type of games children are encouraged to play can have a positive effect on their affective and social behaviour. The children in the cooperative group also appeared to be happy and enjoying themselves. Conversely, children in the competitive games group sometimes appeared quiet and anxious, and were more prone to cheating, pushing and name calling.

We need to ask what we want our children to be. With this type of evidence available, how has the government been able to insist on competitive team games throughout the National Curriculum? The answer lies in political ideology. The National Curriculum was brought into being by a Conservative government that valued the work ethic, the economics of the market place and selection in education. Competitive team games embrace much of this ideology and were therefore a natural choice as a component of physical education. It should be noted that changes are now under way that will liberate the curriculum from this statement of political ideology (see chapter 7).

At Key Stage 2, pupils are expected to work 'alone, in pairs and in groups, and as members of a team'. Again there is some evidence that the development of desirable affective characteristics in this age group can be hindered by competitive sport (Kleiber and Roberts, 1981). These researchers used 4th and 5th graders (9 and 10 year olds) to test the effects of organized sport on social character. They found that some prosocial behaviours in boys may be inhibited by taking part in competitive sport. They also cite research that shows that competition reduces helping and sharing (McGuire and Thomas, 1975), and increases antisocial tendencies (Gelfand and Hartman, 1978). Kleiber and Roberts (1981) conclude by offering suggestions on how to minimize these detrimental effects. First, they suggest that coaches emphasize the 'team' and use team building experiences to promote interdependence. Second, they suggest that players are encouraged to regard opponents as 'associates', without whom the game could not take place. Finally, players should be given more freedom to respond when playing so that natural emotions, such as goodwill and joy, are allowed to show through.

Appreciation of strengths and weaknesses and cooperative team work (again) are all that are mentioned at Key Stage 3. The end-of-Key-Stage-4 description has no affective elements. These extremely limited expectations are at odds with the general requirements for the subject, the beliefs of the many curriculum authorities previously mentioned and also the beliefs of the former prime minister, John Major (Department of National Heritage, 1995), and a former sports minister, Iain Sproat (Spencer, 1994b). However, the new interest in personal, social and health education and the move towards introducing 'citizenship' as a school subject might well prove to be an opportunity to change the current state of affairs.

There is a widely held belief that sport and physical education will inevitably produce good affective characteristics in the participants. So strong is this belief and argument that it was partly responsible for the revisions in the National Curriculum, as elaborated by Iain Sproat (Spencer, 1994b: 8)

> traditional team games . . . teach young people things which so many of them would learn so vividly in no other way; the value of teamwork and team spirit; operating within a framework of rules and laws; good sportsmanship; fair play; commitment; dedication; courage; winning modestly; losing gracefully – in short, the development of good character.

It appears that here again it was being suggested that physical education had a major part to play in the socialization process. This belief in the overwhelming benefits of game playing and competitive activities was pushed to the forefront, in spite of advice to the contrary (Spencer, 1994a). A group of experts explained how girls did not enjoy competition but preferred individual activities and would therefore be disadvantaged by this emphasis. In general girls did not feel as competent as boys at physical education. This advice was largely ignored.

Some of the evidence on the question of whether physical education can achieve these affective outcomes is inconclusive. Greendorfer (1987) summarized the state of research in this area and found that the weight of evidence neither supported nor refuted such claims for physical education. One view is that the subject is a perfect vehicle for personal and social development and that this happens almost as a by-product of good teaching in physical education. The other view is that sports and games too easily promote negative aspects such as elitism, selfishness and division.

A further contradiction is highlighted by the opposing suggestions that pupils' personalities determine their behaviour in class and that their physical education experiences affect their behaviour and development. Does sport build the characters or do sport and physical education attract certain types of characters?

The contradictoriness of these viewpoints and evidence is further compounded by research findings that suggest that, although teachers make some attempt to teach for affective outcomes in their physical education lessons, their pupils do not place much value on these affective outcomes (Ennis, 1985, 1990; Laker 1995b; and Lambdin and Steinhardt, 1992).

While discussing social development through physical activity, Sage (1986) cites developmental scientists and concludes that play has a major role in the early socialization of children. There is a well documented cultural difference between winning and losing in Britain and in the USA. The British notion of modest winners and graceful losers does not travel across the Atlantic. As Sage points out, to be a graceful loser is not something to be admired in the USA. He further suggests that youth sport is merely an element in the cultural reproduction process that produces characteristics that are valued by society, for society.

Gruber (1986) conducted a meta-analysis of eighty-four studies on the effects of physical activity on the self-esteem of elementary school children. He concluded that directed play and physical education do have a positive contribution to make to children's self-esteem. The element of the physical education programme that had the largest effect was physical fitness. Aerobic activities that help children become fitter also help children develop better self-esteem. This provides support for the view that health-related exercise deserves to be more than just a 'theme' in the National Curriculum in physical education. Given current requirements (National Curriculum Council, 1990) health-related exercise does not need to be taught in isolation but could be allowed to permeate all areas of activity. Some schools do teach discrete units on health-related exercise but others do not. Gruber's research indicates that health-related exercise would not only teach children about fitness (cognitive) and help them become fitter (physical), but would also bring benefits to children by enhancing their self-esteem (affective).

Social

The National Curriculum end-of-Key-Stage descriptions make no mention of any social outcomes that might be expected of pupils during their experiences of school curriculum physical education. Bearing in mind the previously demonstrated weight of emphasis given to such elements, this is a glaring inconsistency. Perhaps, in spite of the statement that some such social characteristics were required from physical education, their omission from the end-of-Key-Stage descriptions indicates a recognition that such outcomes may not be measurable, may not be achievable or may not be seen as important.

That pupils have a social agenda and seek social interaction is well documented. Tousignant and Siedentop (1983) investigated some of the interactions that take place in physical education classes. They clearly identified the 'task systems' that Doyle (1979) had originally proposed. First, there was a managerial task system. This was teacher-led and consisted of the administrative and disciplinary functions. Second, there was the instructional task system, which was the teacher's agenda of instructional items to be accomplished during the lesson. Third, there was the transitional task system, consisting of tasks of an organizational nature that allowed the instruction to take place. This task system was later amended to take account of the student-led social agenda that pupils brought to lessons. The systems were thus categorized as managerial (including all organizational functions), instructional and student social. The latter is obviously student-led and dependent to a large degree on how much the teacher is prepared to negotiate between the pupils' social agenda and the instructional agenda. Central to the task system is the manner in which the teacher holds the pupils accountable for actions, efforts and performances. If these are acceptable to the teacher, then some social opportunities may be allowed. Unacceptable instructional and managerial outcomes might severely limit the extent to which the teacher is inclined to allow pupil social behaviour.

This social agenda is prevalent across a number of areas of activity. Perhaps the one that lends itself best to social interaction is 'Outdoor and Adventurous Activities'. Hastie (1995) investigated the 'ecology' of a secondary-school adventure camp in Australia. The 'ecology' of an educational situation is the way in which the tasks and systems interact to facilitate an effective learning experience. Hastie found that the social system was the dominant system and controlled the way in which pupils accomplished the instructional and managerial tasks. The pupils valued three aspects of this system. First, they valued being with friends, as this enhanced the quality of the adventure experience. Second, pupils learned more about their existing friends and also developed social comparisons by making new friends. Last, they enjoyed having fun in their free time. Pupils were able to maximize this free time by performing the instructional tasks well and with great effort. Pupils were also willing to do their household tasks such as cleaning the kitchen so that they could have more time for their social agenda.

Carlson and Hastie (1997) also investigated pupils' social agenda in an Australian secondary school. The pupils concerned were taking part in a sport education unit of work. 'Sport education' is a curriculum model that takes key elements of sports and applies them to the context of physical education. So there are seasons, tournaments, rankings and league tables; pupils have responsibilities for coaching and officiating and there is normally a culminating awards ceremony. Hastie found that more emphasis on teamwork increased opportunities for personal and social development in leadership and cooperation. Winning became more important and led to greater efforts by the pupils. This positive aspect of competition was not detrimental to the less able because they were helped and encouraged by their team-mates to become better players. The pupils had some instructional and managerial responsibilities and these were incorporated into a global task system in which social outcomes were also accepted as an important part. It is clear from this brief account that the pupils had been empowered to take control of their own participation and to some extent of their own learning.

As we saw earlier, our 'socially competent' person has good social skills and interpersonal relationships. These are demonstrated by good social behaviour and social responsibility. Much of the work of Don Hellison has proposed physical education as a vehicle for the development of social responsibility, often in youth categorized as being 'at risk'. Hellison (1978, 1983, 1985, 1987) suggests that physical education can be used as part of an holistic approach to aid personal and social development over a long period, progressing through five levels of responsibility. These levels are labelled by him irresponsibility, self-control, involvement, self-responsibility and caring. Apart from irresponsibility, which is the base level, all characteristics were identified before as being desirable outcomes claimed for physical education but perhaps more difficult to achieve with his 'at-risk' clients. The whole of the programme is designed to improve social skills by using different teacher strategies.

The fact that being in class is a social activity has long been recognized. For teachers and pupils alike education is a social experience. Some subjects allow social interaction more than others. For example, sitting at desks in a classroom limits opportunities for socializing. Moving around a gym or sports hall, however, presents more opportunities for interaction. Physical education is then perhaps the most social of the school subjects.

The research into the social domain of physical education that has been presented so far has described and analysed what goes on in lessons, while Hellison's work describes programmes that are specifically designed to increase social responsibility. Patrick, Ward and Crouch (1998) studied whether pupils could be taught appropriate social behaviours during elementary-school physical education lessons. The teacher strategies they used to motivate good social behaviour were: awarding and removing points; public display of team points; the establishment of a daily point criteria and 'special' activities for successful teams. Taken together these represented a 'good behaviour game'. Appropriate behaviours such as hand shakes, verbal encouragement and thumbs up signs, as well as socially inappropriate behaviour, such as criticism of team-mates, were recorded, to measure the effect of the strategies. They found that pupils learned better social behaviours during the lessons and greatly increased their levels of prosocial behaviours. They also noticed that pupils were more relaxed during the 'game', since they were less likely to be criticized by their peers: playing under the 'good behaviour' conditions was fun.

These reports are part of a growing body of literature that indicate that affective and social behaviours learned in physical education are transferable and can become part of one's character and personality. This should not come as a surprise because we expect the other domains of physical education, the psychomotor and the cognitive, also to teach transferable skills and knowledges.

To answer the rhetorical question posed at the beginning of this section, it seems that we really are expecting physical education to do it all. This will become even more apparent later in this book when we consider the potential of physical education and sport for other arenas of human existence.

4 The Extent of the Affective Dimension in Physical Education

In the last chapter, some of the affective elements commonly claimed for physical education were examined in relation to the nature of the development of the subject. We now turn to the wider affective dimension, involving philosophical, sociological, social developmental and cultural aspects, to ascertain how important the subject is in the development of individuals and also in the development of whole societies. We will see that physical education plays a major role in development both overtly and by means of the 'hidden curriculum'. The affective dimension extends further than is initially obvious and in the course of the chapter the boundaries and areas of that influence will be described and defined.

This book is not the place for a justification of physical education in schools or sport in society. However, it must be recognized that sport dominates the lives of many people: without sport their existence becomes less than whole. Sport enhances and controls the meanings of their lives. When England played Germany in the semi-final of Euro '96 (the European nations football championship), streets were empty. When England played Argentina in the World Cup in 1998 there were record television viewing figures. On both occasions the newspapers next day devoted their front page headlines and stories to the football matches. Famines and wars were relegated to inside pages and the essence of nationhood was epitomized by eleven men playing a game. It is apparent, therefore, that sport is important. And because the content of physical education is largely sport, physical education is also important. The values and attitudes that school children learn through the school subject will affect their view of sport in later life. These attitudes and values will determine whether future World Cups exercise street-emptying influence and whether municipal tennis courts are full during Wimbledon fortnight. In spite of concern over activity levels of youngsters, sport continues to be an important cultural symbol and an important part of many people's lives.

The unique place of sport in the values of modern society attracts much analysis from philosophers, sociologists and popular commentators. A recent trend has been to take a critical attitude towards the nature of sport by pointing out the negative effects of participation, spectatorship and all types of involvement. Unfortunately such critical theorists and commentators have, until very recently, been long on criticism and short on constructive alternatives. A balanced view needs to be taken and it needs to be recognized that sport and physical education offer positive as well as negative features.

A Philosophical View of Sport and Physical Education

The difference between games and play attracts considerable attention from sports philosophers (Morgan and Meier, 1988; Guttman, 1978). Elements that are crucial to play; spontaneity, freedom, the ability to transcend to 'another place' and to adopt different roles; joy; and invention are available in games and sports only in limited versions. Sports and games become codified, framed, bounded and rule-bound. Children obtain messages from games and sports in physical education different from the exuberance and fantasy they get from play.

The joyful running of children in a field all too soon becomes an athletics race in school physical education, and the catching, throwing and hitting games of childhood rapidly become striking and fielding games belonging to the 'Games' area of activity of the National Curriculum. The essence of play, that which makes it so enjoyable, for adults as well as children, should not be lost in the formalization that necessarily takes place when play becomes games, i.e. physical education, and when the informal social interaction of children becomes the formal delivery of education. The joy of sports that is so easily seen in play should be a main objective of teachers and coaches, for, without that joy in children, what hope is there of continued physical activity when the school years are over?

The increasing trend to involve children in structured 'educational' settings at earlier and earlier ages poses the danger of restricting play and replacing it with embryonic physical education. What children play and do with other children is a response to their own needs and their own inclinations. This can be replaced by what adults deem necessary for appropriate development. The imposition of 'acceptable' activities and learning thus begins at an early age. What constitutes play and knowledge is no longer defined by the needs of children at play but is determined by a society that says that young children benefit more from what we, as adults, say is necessary.

There can be no question that children who receive pre-school education have an academic head start over their peers, but at what cost and for what ends? As yet, there is no evidence to suggest that they have an advantage in the area of physical skills. Does the academic advantage continue or are all children levelled in the homogeneous mass of a class? While we must do our best for our children, for they represent the future in all areas of human endeavour, we surely must allow them to be children instead of small versions of adults, to be socialized as soon and as efficiently as possible. It is possible that they know better what they need to do and learn than the adults who control their world.

Huizinga (1955) proposes that civilization works to gradually eliminate play as humans progress through their lives. The inherent characteristics of play, such as fantasy and spontaneity, become untenable in a controlled and conforming society. Work becomes predominant and sport and recreation serve to replace those elements of play that society has taken away from everyday life. This often takes place vicariously, as spectatorship replaces participation.

Just as children develop a sense of who they are and where they fit in with other children socially through play and interaction, so adults are themselves defined partially by their physical activities. This definition of self also encompasses how we perceive ourselves to be viewed by others; the 'looking-glass self'. Thus, what we do for sport, recreation and play says something about us to others. An amateur rugby player triggers a different stereotypical image from a jazzercise participant, and a track and field athlete conjures up a different picture from that suggested by a yachtsman.

A common theme in the varying philosophies of sport is the celebration of sport as a positive, strong and meaningful experience. The 'heroic' nature of participation is elaborated in macho and combative narratives. Sport, maleness and competition become incorporated into a vision of elemental struggle and survival by natural selection, and these notions operate as attractions for a segment of sporting society. Man (including male and female) needs an arena for endeavour, and sport can clearly provide that arena both for participants and for spectators. Taking part in a sailing race, finishing a triathlon, a walk across Dartmoor in winter, or a trek in Nepal are achievable for some people. Watching television pictures of the Round the World Yacht Race in the Southern Ocean, reading about climbing Everest, or watching two top-class rugby teams clash on the sports field are experiences available to almost everyone in western society.

But other philosophical themes can also be identified. Grace, the achievement of beauty in a performance and the development of perfect form and control are an inherent part of many kinds of sport and physical education. The aesthetic nature of some activities is the basis for judgement on the quality of performance: gymnastics, ice skating, synchronized swimming and freestyle skiing are all activities that encompass the aesthetic. Although some sports obviously have the aesthetic as their core, the beauty of human movement can be seen in all sport and physical acticities. The great player Pele called football 'the beautiful game'. This idea of beauty in movement can be applied to any sport, both in the execution of the game as a whole and in the individual performance of a player. A top-class football team can weave fantastic passing patterns, while a pole vaulter can arch fabulously through the air. This beauty is also apparent in humbler settings. A primary-school pupil learning to do a forward roll and a middle-aged man mastering a golf swing may not be stereotypically beautiful, but they undoubtedly emcompass something of the 'nature of what is right' in the attainment of correct form. These are, in their own ways, activities of an aesthetic nature.

Striving for excellence and the crusade to discover the limits of human performance provide another arena for endeavour. This essentially combines the competitive nature of man (but not of all men or women) with sport, producing acts of increasing perfection and ability. As children we are told many times, 'if a thing is worth doing, it's worth doing well'. We are told that we must always do our best. I do not mean to say that this approach is wrong, but it is true that we are conditioned into a competitive mode from a very early age. The natural extension of this is that sport becomes an arena for the demonstration of top-class performances, and part of the avowed purpose of sport is to show the excellence of performance. Gibson (1993) elaborates on this idea and suggests that the values of modern society are so much concerned with measurement, statistics and results that the way we evaluate a performance has been distorted and can now only be viewed in those terms. There is a danger that the subjective appreciation of a good performance, even though it might involve herculean effort, could be replaced by interest merely in the result, and how it measures up to other perormances. This represents a unidimensional view of sport that misses much of what defines sports and games in the field of popular culture. Sports are about more than bare results, just as physical education is about more than just the physical. Perhaps society knows this, and it accounts for the emptiness of the streets during crucial football matches. The emotional experience of watching the whole game and following the rise and fall of fortunes is more valuable than the bland result represented by a scoreline and a list of statistics. To know that 'we lost 2–0' is not the same as experiencing *how* we lost 2–0.

These arenas of 'goodness' present attractive pictures of sport and of sport's potential to be all things to all men. However, not all the pictures are 'good'. Brohm (1978) calls sport a 'prison of measured time', suggesting that the restrictive boundaries of sports performance and the measurement against stringent criteria in fact constitute a sense in which performers are imprisoned within sport. He develops a comprehensive critique of sport and describes its potential for negative effects. The major thrust of Brohm's work is that sport promotes elements of control such as imperialism, economic exploitation, militarism, patriarchy and other forms of hegemony. While it should be noted that Brohm's writing originates in extreme left-wing theory, much of what he says should not be ignored, as it presents a counter to the positive images of sport. In criticizing sport as a tool of functionalist ideology, Brohm makes the case that sport prepares workers for production in a capitalist society by teaching the values of hard work and conformity. Professional sport provides a spectacle for the masses and regulates and socializes aggression by offering acceptable outlets for violence. (We might ask here if efforts to control football hooligans pay any more than lip service to the idea of law and order, or whether such controlled violence is covertly tolerated by the authorities as a safety valve for unrest caused by poor social conditions and high unemployment.)

Britain's export of sport to the world was a product of its imperial expeditions to many parts of the globe. Brohm claims that sport therefore contains and promotes the values of imperialism. The patriarchal hegemony of the Victorian era, in which men exercised control over all aspects of life in society, except raising children and running the home, was embedded in the idea of empire, and sport played a part in supporting those values.

Whether we agree nowadays with this view is not the point. What is important is that many of these negative aspects suggested by Brohm were taken up at the time by critical theorists and called the 'hidden curriculum' of school physical education (Bain, 1975). This idea of a hidden agenda for the school subject has continued to be popular with writers (Bain, 1985 and Fernandez-Balboa, 1993) and still contains a credible account of some of the possibilities of physical education. This theme is taken up and elaborated later in this chapter.

Summary of the philosophical view

The importance of play and the aura of wonder, fun and awe that surrounds play, are all attainable in physical education. To lose the emotional attachment that is part of play is to reduce physical education to mere mechanical exercise. Concentration on the psychomotor and the technical at the expense of the affective unnecessarily restricts children's appreciation and enjoyment of sport. Dibbo and Gerry (1995) make a good case for the holistic education of the child through physical education so that children will have the ability to understand and appreciate the whole experience of physical activity for themselves. They suggest that a physical education programme that limits itself solely to the physical is reverting to a dualist position where the body is seen as separate from the child. What it is to become emotionally involved and to understand emotional involvement should not be lost from play when it becomes physical education. This emotional involvement consists not simply of the tears of losing but also of appreciation of the real and deep feelings that physical activity can generate and which add considerably to the enjoyment of that activity and the understanding of one's own participation in it.

Challenge, and sport and physical education as endeavour, need to be incorporated into the school subject. The benefits of facing and overcoming a realistically set challenge have long been recognized by proponents of outdoor education, which appears in the National Curriculum as an area of activity, Outdoor and Adventurous Activities (O&AA). Other areas of the physical education curriculum can also contribute to challenge but sometimes their potential is overshadowed because O&AA is so obviously well placed to provide this experience for children.

Aesthetics can too easily be seen as the sole preserve of the gymnast or the dancer. But should teachers not express appreciation of beauty in all areas of physical activity? A fluent running action contains the same elements of perfection as the sequence of a poised gymnast. Unfortunately, some teachers, particularly men, are uncomfortable with this expression of aesthetics. It would be a shame if this opportunity were lost to children because of teachers' inhibitions. Perhaps the next generation, of more enlightened teachers, will be less bound by such stereotypes.

Measurement of performance, rather than judgement of performance, and the competitive nature of sports are ideally suited to the nature of physical education. However, we must consider Gibson's warning (1993). The values that measurement and competition promote must be tempered by an appreciation that the experience of physical education involves more than just winning and performance. The way a performance is achieved can be as important as its result.

A Sociological View of Sport and Physical Education

A sociological perspective of education is incomplete without some analysis of the place, potential and purpose of physical education and school sport in the whole school curriculum. Sport does not exist in a vacuum in society. Sport interacts with the other institutions in society just as individuals interact with each other. The sociology of sport and physical education is well supported by a large body of literature whose function is to analyse, interpret and explain these interactions of institutions and individuals. For the purposes of this commentary I will draw on that literature and synthesize what is relevant to sport and physical education. The consideration of sport and physical education from a sociological point of view is more easily managed if the discussion is split into 'macro' issues and 'micro' issues.

Macro issues are those that explore the relationships between and within large societal institutions. These are institutions such as the church, politics and sport and education. So the place of politics in sport would be a macro issue, as would the way education is used to socialize children.

Micro issues concentrate more on the effect that participation has on the development of the individual. So social development aspects such as the development of self-esteem through physical activity can be seen to be micro issues.

Politics and sport

Political involvement in physical education is discussed later but the way in which politics uses sport merits a brief mention here as it falls within the area of sport sociology. Olympic boycotts, control of funding, politicians' efforts to be associated with successful sportspersons (probably more noticeable in the USA than in Britain or Europe) and the importance, or lack of it, placed on sport all tell us something of the political climate towards sport.

Politicians use sport when it suits them. Margaret Thatcher's partially successful British boycott of the 1980 Moscow Olympics was merely an expedient measure to show solidarity with the USA and President Reagan. The nominal reason for the boycott was the USSR's invasion of Afghanistan but this should be seen against the background of the Cold War, in which conflicting ideologies were seeking to establish superiority. At other times Thatcher virtually ignored sport in political terms.

Senior political figures are often seen at major sporting venues. The FA Cup Final, cricket Test Matches, and Rugby Internationals all attract politicians who want to be associated with something that people regard as a major contribution to the fabric of their lives. John Major's love of cricket often led to him being seen at matches, which certainly did his public image no harm. It helped him to foster an association with the common man; of all the recent Conservative prime ministers his image was closest to that of an ordinary man. American Presidents meet Olympic gold medal winners and telephone the dressing rooms of Superbowl winners. This can be interpreted as a desire to be seen as part of something successful.

In addition to his enjoyment of cricket, John Major adopted school sport as a rallying point for the nation. He promised to put sport back at the heart of school life (Department of National Heritage, 1995), though there is considerable evidence that sport was in fact never far away from the heart of school life (Gilroy and Clarke, 1997). His intention, which was acted upon, was that competitive team games should constitute the major part of the National Curriculum in physical education. He had a personal and political belief that such activities promoted and instilled traits that were socially desirable and necessary for the functioning of a modern capitalist society.

Not all political involvement in sport should be sneered at. The huge success of the National Lottery in terms of raising money for good causes has tremendously benefited the provision of sports facilities. Questions may be asked about the distribution of some of the funding but it is undoubtedly true that facilities in general have increased and improved.

Sport and gender

A common criticism of the National Curriculum in physical education is that it is not free from gender bias (Flintoff, 1991 and Talbot, 1996). Talbot (1993) identifies four problem areas: the perceived low status of activities associated with girls; reluctance to focus on the source of the problem; failure to question the place of physical education in promoting a male-dominated ideology; and reluctance to acknowledge physical education's influence in promoting that dominant ideology. The perceived low status of activities associated with girls has been further exacerbated by the ever-present strand of competitive team games running through the National Curriculum (Department of National Heritage, 1995). It has been demonstrated that girls prefer activities that do not focus on competition and teams but on cooperation and also that they prefer individual activities (Milosevic, 1996). Put simplistically, while boys might like to play football, girls might prefer aerobics or gymnastics (Williams, 1989). (This illustration itself represents the stereotypes that are so easily attached to sporting behaviour, even with the best of motives.)

The gender bias of sport and physical education, and the male hegemony that results are the subject of much sociological literature (Hargreaves, 1994; Clarke and Humberstone, 1997). It could be argued that physical education and sport are merely playing their parts within the total education system in socializing children into society. We should not be surprised, therefore, that although equality of opportunity is avowed in the National Curriculum, there are identifiable elements that are clearly unequal.

Experience in America is not dissimilar. 'Title IX' was made law in 1972, in an attempt to bring women's sport in education environments out of the shadow of the male varsity sports structure, and to ensure that women were given equal opportunities for sports participation. But both Sage (1990) and Coakley (1994) make strong cases that inequality continues to affect women in American sport. They cite the patriarchal hegemony prevalent in many western societies, and a series of myths that maintain women's subordinate position. These myths suggest that women are physiologically unsuited to sport because of their childbearing role and perceived differences in performance abilities, as well as sociologically unsuited because of the perceptions that society has of a woman's role, coupled with the perceived inappropriateness of sports for women.

Sport and class

When Brohm (1978) suggested that one of sport's functions was to condition individuals so that they became useful members of society in terms of units of production in a labour force, he was expressing the view of critical theorists, that sport classifies, stratifies and discriminates. We have already briefly explored the aspect of gender discrimination. Let us now look at the idea that sport and physical education maintain a class structure and reinforce the class boundaries apparent in our society.

Certain sporting occasions conjure up images of well-heeled sections of society at frivolous play: strawberries and cream at Wimbledon; the striped blazers and boaters at Henley; and champagne and the Royal Yacht Squadron in Cowes Week. Other sports result in different mental pictures: masses crowded together on the terraces of football grounds (no longer a valid image of English football!); a cheering crowd at a professional darts competition; and the flat caps of spectators at a dog racing track. The whole social structure of this country is so steeped in the divisions of class that stereotypes such as these have some meaning for most people, whether or not they are still true.

Much of what we are and what we will become is determined by 'class chances', an idea that suggests that only a limited amount of choice is available to any one class. Class is obviously determined by many factors such as family background, environment, wealth and education. This is still somewhat true in sport. The ability or inclination to go skiing is limited to some of the population, just as the ability or inclination to visit a speedway track is limited to others. But this is not the only way that sport can perpetuate class differences. Many sports originated in and were codified by a social elite: baseball in the USA and cricket in England are good examples of this. Early clubs were a result of patronage by the wealthy and access to them was severely restricted. Access to clubs and thus to some sporting opportunities is still controlled by those who run the clubs. There is also an economic barrier; although one may legitimately have access to the sports and the clubs, it is limited in practical terms by the costs involved in being a member, buying equipment and the non-working time needed to take part in the sport.

Sport is often seen as a vehicle for social mobility: work hard at your sport, become successful and you will climb the social and economic ladder and it is often true that social mobility is enhanced by club membership. But as far as the activity itself is concerned, Sage (1990) points out that in the USA only 1 in 10,000 male high school athletes (referring to all sports representatives) is likely to become a professional sportsman. The chances for women are even slimmer because there are so few professional sports for women. So although sport promotes the work ethic, it is unlikely to allow real social or economic mobility in a society where class affiliation has more to do with family and education than with sports ability.

Critical theory and functionalism

Much of the above will be recognized as taking a left-wing critical theorist's viewpoint. This is a view of the world that identifies inequality, privilege, control and elitism as major components in a hegemonic society that seeks to maintain the status quo at the expense of individual opportunity and self-expression. When applied to sport and physical education, this manifests itself as a view that looks mainly at what is wrong with the way things are. It must be remembered that this is only one interpretation of the workings of society. In simple terms, as this is not a sociology text, a structural functionalist approach, for example, would take the different view that the structure and stability of society depends upon certain frameworks being maintained. So the argument concerning political intervention might instead be couched in terms of support for sport, value for money and attempting to do the best with limited resources, while giving the country what it wants, i.e. competitive national teams, access to facilities and a curriculum that prepares children to become useful members of society.

The functionalist case regarding gender states that inequities are decreasing and that the National Curriculum is meant to be 'broad and balanced', the fact that it is not, being due to teachers failing to implement it properly. Although women are encouraged to participate in sport, they cannot ignore their roles as childbearers and family carers. The fact that women's sport is severely under-represented in terms of media coverage is the price we pay in a free society. The public decide what they want to see and the newspapers, radio, TV and other media outlets provide it.

Functionalists argue that with the advent of comprehensive education, the vast majority of the population have equal opportunities to experience a good education, and, within that a standardized physical education, so that the notion of 'class chances' is virtually eliminated. Nobody is stopped from going to Wimbledon or Cowes on the basis of class: people merely make choices from an open menu about what sporting activities they want to view and take part in.

The way you choose to understand the potential of sport from a macro-sociological perspective really depends on your political viewpoint. It is not a question of one view being proved and the other disproved, but more a question of opinion about how society works. The foregoing discussion merely describes two different approaches to sport and physical education in the macro-sociological context.

A Social Development View of Sport and Physical Education

In what ways can physical education help in the social development of children, and what can it offer individuals in schools? There is an assumption that involvement in games, sports and recreation inevitably leads to good and productive outcomes. John Major obviously believed this, as do many decision makers and educators without any background in empirical research. However, as Greendorfer (1987: 59) suggests, 'This assumption has led to the unfaltering belief that organised physical activity provides a medium through which culturally valued personal and social attitudes, behaviors and values can be (automatically) transferred to other spheres of social life'. Greendorfer's paper calls into question the validity of much of the evidence that sports involvement is beneficial, by highlighting methodological problems with various studies. The evidence on whether or not sport and physical education promote affective development was inconclusive (Greendorfer, 1987), but this has not stopped many authors writing on the subject. The belief in the inherent social good of sports and physical education appears to be alive and well.

The affective domain in physical education consists of a number of characteristics, attitudes and values that curriculum documents, teachers and authors claim can be promoted by taking part in physical activity. A simple comprehensive list of these characteristics, attitudes and values serves no purpose as each then exists in isolation, having no apparent relationship to any other. A better way of handling the affective domain is to develop a conceptual framework into which all characteristics, attitudes and values can be accommodated. It is a useful tool that allows us to organize these ideas in a meaningful, more manageable way.

Categorization of characteristics

Laker (1996) sought to build a three-dimensional framework which would enable student teachers to design their lessons and teaching to take more account of the affective domain. The three dimensions were: the affective traits, teaching strategies and types of activity. Individual affective traits such as teamwork and fair play were put into generic groups of traits.

Figure 4.1 Generic groupings of individual traits

So it can be seen from figure 4.1 that fair play, honesty, peer support, peer respect and competitiveness were grouped together as 'sportsmanship' traits. Obviously, many of the individual traits could appear in several generic groups. This duplication did not pose a problem for the development of the framework as it was only intended to be a mechanism to facilitate decisions regarding interaction of the three dimensions and the practicalities of lesson planning. The interaction of the three dimensions determined what activity was taught, using which strategy, to achieve what affective outcome. So, for example, a student might decide to teach volleyball (activity) using teacher talk and discussion (strategy) to promote teamwork (affective outcome) within the generic group of 'cooperation'. No attempt was made to define the various traits. This is not a problem at the practical level because there are commonly held views among teachers about what is meant by 'sportsmanship' or by 'teamwork', for example. Small differences in the perceived meanings of terms do not change these commonly held ideas, nor do they matter in terms of teaching.

The issue of definitions is addressed by Gibbons and Bressan (1991). Although they provide another useful conceptual framework (figure 4.2) for the teaching of the affective domain, the main focus of their discussion is on defining the terms used. They suggest that teachers consider two areas for development: first, there is the area of moral attitudes (figure 4.3); second, there is the area of aesthetic attitudes (figure 4.4). As can be seen, each of these sub-domains contains a cluster of traits in the same way as Laker's framework. So the moral sub-domain consists of 'autonomy', 'altruism' and 'responsibility'. 'Autonomy' is further sub-divided into self-respect, self-discipline, self-reliance and self-confidence. Each of these characteristics is explained and defined. Neither Laker's nor Gibbons and Bressan's framework deals with the problem of assessment of the affective, but their definitions will prove valuable when assessment is considered. We must be able to define something if we are to be able to measure it effectively. Taken together, these two frameworks provide a good working

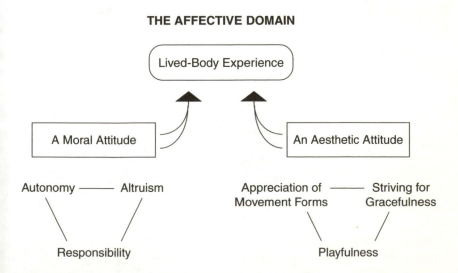

THE AFFECTIVE DOMAIN

Lived-Body Experience

A Moral Attitude   An Aesthetic Attitude

Autonomy ——— Altruism

Responsibility

Appreciation of ——— Striving for
Movement Forms   Gracefulness

Playfulness

Figure 4.2 Content of the affective domain as it relates to physical education

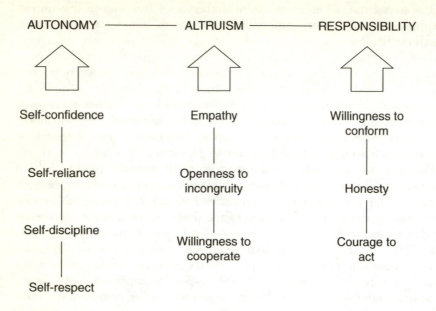

Figure 4.3 Concepts and content focuses for the development of a moral attitude

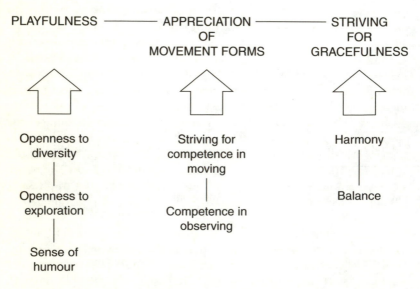

Figure 4.4 Concepts and content focuses for the development of an aesthetic attitude

model to aid the implementation of strategies for teaching in a way that accommodates the affective domain, rather than having it tagged on as an afterthought.

Possibilities for social development

This look at conceptual frameworks does not answer the question raised at the start of the chapter about whether sport and physical education really do have a social development role to play. However, it does suggest that there is potential to achieve social development objectives. It is my contention that the evidence is inconclusive in this area because school sport has not been structured with social development in mind. Lip service is paid to the idea that sport is 'character building' and there will be talk about representing the school, developing self-esteem and so on. But what type of character does it build if over-enthusiastic parents shout advice to 'take him out' at a primary-school seven-a-side football match? And how is self-esteem developed when a child cries because he did not win a race; not because he came last, but because he did not win? How much better it would have been for the primary school football players to have tried their best and enjoyed the game despite the result; to have shaken hands at the end and praised their opponents' efforts, and to have come away thinking, 'that was fun, I'd like to do that again sometime soon'. And how much better it would have been for the second-place sprinter to have congratulated the winner and then determined to have found out more about running and training so that he might improve his performance next time.

Physical education is not taught with social development in mind. The National Curriculum in physical education and teacher training courses in physical education place the most emphasis on the performance side of the subject. Physical education is obviously concerned with sport and physical performance but, if it claims to have a social development role, it must not be exclusively about physical performance. If this blinkered concentration continues then a wonderful opportunity to help young people in our society is being missed. The knowledges and attitudes needed to encourage our youngsters into healthy, active lifestyles are not being taught. All that is being taught are the skills, and alone they are not enough. Young people deserve to enjoy their physical education, and they need to know the benefits of activity. Knowledge of where and how they can take part in physical activity coupled with a positive attitude and enthusiasm will encourage the continuation of an active lifestyle.

The 'Standards for the Award of Qualified Teacher Status' (Teacher Training Agency, 1997: 4) now require that new teachers will 'understand how pupils' learning in the subject is affected by their physical, intellectual, emotional and social development'. They must also be able to 'plan opportunities to contribute to pupils' personal, spiritual, moral, social and cultural development' (p. 7). These are requirements for all subjects, not just physical education. Will practising teachers and training institutions take notice of this and actually incorporate it into their teaching and initial teacher training or will they continue merely to pay lip service to it? If they were to do this then a big step will have been taken towards effectively developing this part of physical education.

Research evidence

Although a large body of evidence neither supports nor refutes the proposition that physical education could have a social development component, much of that evidence is outdated. The more recent action research projects suggest that the promotion of a social development component is a possibility.

Grineski (1989) claimed that positive, or negative, social outcomes can be achieved depending on how the games are structured. Grineski found that kindergarten children showed a total of 230 'prosocial' behaviours of which 228 were associated with cooperatively structured games. Grineski concluded that young children are capable of exhibiting prosocial behaviour interactions during games participation and that this is more likely to happen in games of a cooperative nature. The researchers also reported that during the cooperatively structured games, pupils appeared to be happy and enjoying themselves. During the competitively structured games, on the other hand, the pupils appeared quiet and anxious and even exhibited anti-social behaviour such as cheating, pushing and name calling.

The suggestion follows that to encourage prosocial behaviours, teachers will need to modify existing games or invent new games, to concentrate on the development of these behaviours. The obvious problem is that the nature of most sports and games is competitive, and under the constraints of the National Curriculum the opportunity for the use of alternative games is severely limited.

Sportsmanship, or prosocial, curriculum models have received some research attention. Sharpe, Brown and Crider (1995) tested the effectiveness of their curriculum model using three elementary classes in Lincoln, Nebraska in the USA. The pupils had poor social skills, demonstrated by the high incidence of disciplinary measures taken with these classes. The researchers included a control group, the lack of which was one of Greendorfer's (1987) main criticisms of many studies in this field. They not only tested the effectiveness of their interventions but also investigated whether the outcomes carried over into normal classroom settings. The intervention strategies consisted mainly of teacher talk, encouragement, setting of objectives and verbal feedback on progress. The behaviours targeted for improvement were teacher-independent sport conflict resolution, off-task behaviour and increased leadership and support behaviours in the context of participation in a team sport. Results showed an immediate increase in pupil leadership and independent conflict resolution, and an increase in time devoted to participation caused by a decrease in the frequency of pupil off-task behaviours. Importantly, similar changes in pupil behaviour were also observed in classroom settings. This could have consequences for the promotion of physical education as a means of helping children develop and maintain socially acceptable traits not only in physical education classes and school, but perhaps in a variety of locations.

These two studies clearly demonstrate that physical education, taught in a certain way, can encourage prosocial behaviour and discourage antisocial behaviour in primary school-age children. Grineski's (1989) study suggests that young primary school children might be better off with activities of a cooperative nature rather than beginning their school lives by being exposed to team sports competition. Sharpe, Brown and Crider's (1995) work hints at a bigger role for physical education in the social development area. This will be examined further in relation to personal, social and moral education and also in relation to the notion of holistic education for citizenship.

Most of the research into the possibility of social development through physical education and sports participation has been conducted in primary schools. The reason for this is not clear. It may be that primary school teachers have more control over how they organize their classes and therefore various experimental interventions can be more easily accommodated. Secondary school settings are more restricted by curriculum requirements and timetable structures. In spite of this, Carlson and Hastie (1997) managed to investigate how pupils socialized in physical education classes in a high school in Australia. Three classes were being taught using the sport education curriculum model (Siedentop, 1994). This model was developed in the USA in the early 1980s in an attempt to make physical education more relevant and authentic for the participants. Pupils are affiliated to a team for a season and take responsibility within the team. Matches are played, records kept and there is usually a concluding tournament. Teaching and coaching, although led and directed by the teacher, are done in team groups. So the normal teacher roles of instructing and managing are to some extent adopted by the pupils. The authors reported that some affective outcomes had been achieved by the pupils. They learned something of leadership skills, communication was enhanced and a certain amount of trust was developed. There was an increased emphasis on competition but, because the season was longer than a normal teaching unit, low and average skilled pupils had more chance to improve. This enabled them to view the competitive element more positively. They also learned the value of teamwork, and this, along with a lack of selfishness, developed over the course of the season.

A growing body of evidence indicates that sport education as a physical education curriculum model has much to commend it. It appears that teachers and pupils like it and there are increased levels of active participation. The recent and current literature suggests that physical education, including school sport, has the potential to go 'beyond the boundaries' of physical education and sport in the area of social development. The few research projects that have been reported here confirm that potential. Unfortunately, in general that potential is not being recognized and an enormous opportunity is being missed.

A Cultural View of Sport and Physical Education

A culture is a system of shared values, meanings and symbols that enables societies and individuals to operate without continually redefining circumstances and situations. 'Culture' refers to the way institutions and individuals work to produce and reproduce those common elements that are central to the functioning of society. For example, sport is a symbol or institution to which is attached a shared meaning. We recognize sport without having to define it. We recognize that ballroom dancing is not sport, but football is; that driving to work is not sport, but motor racing is. There is a cultural and popular definition of what sport is. Hargreaves (1986) argues that these definitions vary in different cultural settings and even between sub-cultures of the same dominant culture. This leads us to differentiations within an overall culture, so we have popular culture, black culture, and so on. It is possible that sport means different things in each of these sub-cultures and that the value placed on sport will change with its definition. So participation in sport for a group of hill-walkers will mean things like freedom from everyday worries, a natural experience and closeness to the elements. For a group taking part in an aerobics class, however, sport might have connotations such as health promotion, body image, socializing and fitness. People take part in sport and physical activity because it means positive things to them. They perceive a benefit from it. (This even applies to professional sportspeople who take part in sport for monetary gain, where the most obvious positive meaning for them is the provision of an income.)

In a similar way, we all have a view of what 'education' means. We have all experienced schooling as children, we experience it again through our children, and we pass on our interpretation of the meaning of education. This interpretation is similar to most other people's and therefore the meaning is reinforced. We do not have to explain what we mean every time we use the word. Moreover, there is a form of education that is acceptable to the culture, and that form, or type of education, is what the common definition describes.

Kirk and Tinning (1990) make a very strong case for physical activity programmes in educational institutions being instrumental in promoting a validated form of socially acceptable sport and human movement. Physical education in schools begins to form our common definition of what activity, sport and recreation are. The National Curriculum is a good example of a selection of activities that is deemed appropriate by an authoritative group of people. The selection implies values and levels of importance that are of benefit to some – we hope most – but are, nevertheless, detrimental to others. Society, or rather a dominant segment of society, has constructed an authorized view of school sport and physical education and this has become embedded in our culture to such an extent that, when challenged, the authorities react by strongly imposing their view. This was demonstrated when teachers challenged the emphasis on competitive team games in the National Curriculum. The claim was that it did not lead to a 'broad and balanced' curriculum. The response came in the form of *Sport: Raising the Game* (Department of National Heritage, 1995) in which the intention was stated that sport should return to the heart of school life: the authorized version had been imposed.

Sport as celebration

I am attracted by the interpretation of sport as a celebration and perhaps that is what the culture of sport and physical education should be; a celebration of activity, a celebration of sport, and a celebration of life. The interference of politicians, the critical analysis of theorists and the negative potential of sport in society and the subject in schools, should not be allowed to detract from the reality of the euphoric feelings and the glorious meanings that bind people to their sports and to each other. (For a wonderful illustration of these emotions see Inglis, 1977.) Simply put, sport brings joy to those who accept its challenge. It can also bring sadness and frustration, but of such a type that they can be seen as part of a greater joy in which the bitter taste of disappointment allows the sweetness of satisfaction to be truly appreciated. Perhaps sport is needed in our culture to provide an avenue for that celebration; there is no other aspect of human endeavour that provides this opportunity in quite the same way. It is said that religion exists because man needs an outlet for the expression of faith. In a similar way, sport and recreation might exist because man needs to express the peculiar celebration of the human body, human movement and the human spirit.

Some of the qualities that are encompassed within sport are used as metaphors in everyday life. Some of these are bits of 'goodness' that are taken from the playing field, often out of context, and used to explain or emphasize a point in daily existence. So, we exhort our fellow men to 'play the game' in an effort to ensure fair treatment, or we suggest that he 'plays with a straight bat' when we mean someone is correct, honest and forthright. Conversely, someone is 'for the high jump' when they are in trouble, and when a person is 'thrown a loop', they have a difficult, unexpected situation to deal with. These phrases drawn from sport demonstrate that much of the language of sport is part of common usage and therefore has a shared meaning that does not have to be reinterpreted each time it is used.

Hargreaves (1986) points out that different cultures can attribute different meanings to the same situations or practices and that this exaggerates cultural diversity even within a given society. The way in which a sport is played can be determined by cultural background. Thus there is a difference between cricket played in an English public school and cricket played on a West Indian beach. The game in the English public school contains ritual, custom and tradition, whereas the common image of a West Indian beach game would include exuberance, elaborate skill and much joy and laughter. Nevertheless, the participants in both these games might take them equally seriously, in spite of the differences in what it means to them to be playing cricket.

The language of sport, not just the words and phrases, but what sport means to people is an important currency. It often eases the path of everyday encounters. 'Did you see the game last night?', is safe ground, and a ground on which otherwise disparate participants can communicate. This type of social discourse is often called small talk, but it lubricates the mechanism of social interaction by providing a common ground. As Inglis (1977) shows, sport also provides some cultural histories and stories that are told and retold, so becoming part of legend. The rehearsal of these stories, often to the same audience, adds a patina to them such that they can take their place in tradition. If one view of sport as an important part of culture were to be emphasized, I believe this to be one of the most powerful. It shapes our ideas of sporting tradition as a part of a common culture and it provides the substance of that tradition, becoming part of a comfortable contentment that can enthuse, invigorate and inspire us long after an event has happened and long after the 'actors' have lost the physical capabilities to reenact the scene: the myth becomes as important as the act. So sporting achievements and stories become part of a cultural fabric.

The Hidden Curriculum

'The hidden curriculum' refers to what is taught to pupils by the way the school operates, by the way the teachers behave and by the interactions that take place on a daily basis in schools. The concept of a hidden curriculum is firmly located in the work of critical theorists. The earlier look at the negative potential of sport and physical education drew mostly on the work of Brohm to illustrate a critical view of their contribution to society (see pp. 35–36). (This was briefly balanced there with a functionalist description of sport in which the arguments that might be put to counter the critical perspective were suggested.)

Education clearly has a formal and open curriculum. This is what is overtly taught to pupils. In terms of subject knowledge, the National Curriculum is a good example of this. It is easy to see what schools are required to teach to pupils. Each subject has its own body of knowledge that is deemed important enough to be formalized into the school curriculum. It is timetabled into the school day and is in the public domain for all to see. But the school curriculum does not consist only of what is taught in lessons. Field trips, sports fixtures, plays, concerts and open days are examples of the activities included in this broader definition of the curriculum of the school. By their inclusion, the school and the education system are saying something about their value. Field trips and visits generally enrich and add to the experience of the subjects for the pupils: they are chances to see in real life what has been explained in the classroom. Sports fixtures, plays and concerts are celebrations of excellence and chances for the better performers to test and exhibit their skills in a wider context. Individuals, schools and society know this and approve of it. These things contribute to the whole school curriculum, or at least the curriculum that is seen.

But there is another side to the curriculum that is not so obvious or clear. By spending eleven years or frequently more in school, young people absorb certain messages. What those messages are depends on many factors, but the messages are usually those that are 'approved' by society.

This begins with the structure of the school. Are children grouped according to their abilities? If so, what does this mean to the children? To those in more able groups it indicates that they have better abilities and will receive a more advanced version of the knowledge than those in other groups. To those in the less able groups, it means that they are not as able as the other children and they will receive a version that is easier to understand, a watered down and adjusted version of the real thing. There are very good reasons for teaching ability groups, but messages such as those above will inevitably be conveyed in those situations.

The wearing of a school uniform and school PE kit also promotes certain values. On the positive side it can develop a pride in the school and a sense of belonging. A compulsory PE uniform allows the teachers to impose appropriate safety requirements and ensures that the children are wearing clothing suitable for the activity. It also stops the teasing of pupils who do not have the 'correct' replica shirts of fashionable clubs. However, individuals become part of a homogeneous group, individuality is suppressed and conforming with the majority is seen to be important.

The 'uniform' that the teachers wear also says something about their position in the school, their function as a role model, and the way they want to be treated by the pupils and by other members of staff. 'Smart' clothes are the norm. This usually means ties for men and skirts or smart slacks for women. Physical education teachers wear tracksuits or shorts, sometimes games skirts for women, and sports shirts. In the classroom and in the sports hall teachers wear a version of what the pupils wear. There is some variety, but not much: teachers' dress is almost as closely controlled as that of the pupils. Teachers are willingly, and usually knowingly, contributing to the messages of the hidden curriculum. (For readers from countries other than the UK, a discussion of school uniform may well be alien to their experience of school life. The wearing of school uniform is mostly limited to the United Kingdom and some other Commonwealth countries. One could pose the question why, if the wearing of school uniform is so beneficial, has it not been adopted worldwide?)

These two examples, timetable organization and what the people in the school wear, are perhaps the most obvious. The hidden curriculum, however, operates on many levels and in many ways. The pupils also have a part to play in establishing a status quo and their reactions to, and treatment of, other pupils clearly demonstrates what they think is important and what their sub-cultural norms and values are.

The idea of how girls should behave and how boys should behave is one of the areas where the structure of school, teachers' behaviour and pupils' treatment of others contribute to the hidden curriculum. It has been suggested earlier that this has been institutionalized into the structure of the National Curriculum. In the following argument, gender differentiation is used as an example of the hidden curriculum at work. In a patriarchal society, sport has very strong connotations of maleness. Bain (1985) suggests that the social construction of what is 'feminine' and what is 'masculine' is rehearsed and further defined in sport and physical education. Fernadez-Balboa (1993) agrees when he states that physical education is discriminatory in many areas, gender being one of them. He lists race, socio-economic status, physical ability and intellectual level as being other areas that are the subject of discrimination in physical education. It is well known that teachers, perhaps inadvertently, pay more attention to boys in class and that in mixed-sex classes girls get less opportunity to take an active part because of boys' domination of the games and of the space.

This problem is not confined to the structure of the curriculum, the way the subject is delivered and the way teachers teach: the pupils themselves operate a system of discrimination in lessons. This was recognized by Kirk (1995) in an account of the application of action research to real-life teaching situations. A female student teacher undertook a project to teach tag rugby to a mixed-sex class of fourteen year olds in an attempt to overcome the dominant male orientation associated with team games, particularly rugby. Initially, there was resistance from both boys and girls: the boys were resentful at having to play with the girls, as they considered it 'below them' and detrimental to their games; the girls did not enjoy the way in which their lack of skill prevented them taking a full part in the games, nor did they enjoy the way in which the boys physically dominated the game. After many interventions, the situation improved somewhat, although it did not reach a point where both boys and girls were equally or fully involved in the lessons: boys still dominated.

This type of pupil behaviour was further confirmed by Loadman (1998) in his ethnographic account of incidents in a primary physical education lesson. In one example, pupils were asked to 'find a partner'. All the children paired off with partners of the same sex, leaving one boy, Jim. Other boys suggested that he paired off with the remaining girl, while exchanging smiles and looks. The analysis that followed suggested that Jim was not included in the boys' culture. First, he did not wear the acceptable clothing (here we have a case in favour of school PE uniform). Instead of an England,

Manchester United or Arsenal football shirt, Jim was dressed in a creased aertex T-shirt. Second, Jim was not athletically built, in fact he was quite heavy. Jim did not conform in any way to the definition of masculinity that had been constructed by the sub-culture of the boys in the class. He did not have the right kind of body, nor did he possess the 'street cred' that the right kind of kit would confer.

These two examples of the use and application of the norms of pupil culture clearly illustrate that it is not the educational hierarchy that is solely responsible for the imposition of a hidden curriculum. The pupils, in their own way, have the power to define what is and what is not acceptable in their culture. They can very easily use their own power relationships to develop and impose a hidden curriculum.

Fernandez-Balboa and the hidden curriculum

One of the leading commentators on the state of physical education in the USA is Fernandez-Balboa (1993). His critical analysis of the way physical education is framed and taught in schools is a comprehensive and condemnatory piece of work. A detailed look at each component of his analysis will illustrate the perceived power of physical education and school sport to promote one sociological viewpoint. I will also attempt to relate his commentary to the British context and evaluate the appropriateness of his comments here. We have already seen how Fernandez-Balboa suggests physical education is discriminatory by using gender as an example (see p. 48). He also points out the stratified hierarchical and competitive nature of the subject by noting that competitive team games have been given a privileged place in the school curriculum. Even in Britain, competitive team games are placed above all other sports and physical education activities. Results are read out in assemblies and head teachers use any sporting successes to promote their schools in the competitive environment of parental choice. This also supports the claim that sport and physical education are elitist: those that take part in the privileged sports are elite participants.

It is self-evident that people who take part in sport know that they put their peformance on display and that it is easy to see the quality of their performance. However, in the context of a physical education lesson, it would be wrong to make those pupils who are not in the elite stratum feel inferior. Unfortunately, this feeling of inferiority is very common and it has a detrimental effect on the self-esteem of some children.

Fernandez-Balboa also claims that physical education is uncontextual and impersonal; that it has very little relevance to many children's lives outside school. Here it could be argued that part of the aim of the subject is to enable pupils to live more fulfilling lives when they leave school and that, although the activities may start as uncontextual, they can become more meaningful in later life. However, these connections are difficult for the children themselves to make.

Fernandez-Balboa's continuing argument claims that education, and therefore physical education, is not value free; it is not apolitical. Physical education does not exist in a vacuum, being part of the 'official' knowledge that is imparted in schools. It has already been claimed that this 'official' knowledge carries the endorsement of dominant groups seeking to impose an 'authorized version' of physical education. Fernandez-Balboa further suggests that the way the subject is currently taught, at least in the USA, is restrictive, fragmented, linear and logical, reproductive, coercive and eliminative. These descriptors echo the works of Basil Berstein (1975). Berstein makes the case that knowledge acquisition and progression through the subject knowledge's hierarchies are restricted by the barriers and hurdles that confront one along the way. This is institutionally implemented by the structures of schools and examinations and by the political nature of curriculum design. It also means that certain 'bits' of knowledge are packaged for consumption, and must be consumed in a certain order. So, in Britain, class grades, GCSEs, A levels and degrees are usually taken sequentially. Along the way, those who do not master the skills and knowledges that are required are eliminated and will remain at a certain level unless they can find ways of circumventing the barrier. (For example, students who fail A levels will be unable to enter university unless they take an 'access' course which provides an alternative route into higher education.) Knowledge distribution is based on a pyramid principle. There is a broad base of knowledge available to all, but this is followed by increasingly narrower bands of knowledge available to those who reach higher up the pyramid by successfully clearing the barriers placed in their way. Fernandez-Balboa's interpretation of Berstein's work illustrates that this is as true for physical education as it is for other subjects and for education as a whole.

Fernandez-Balboa's claim that physical education is coercive is made clearer when coercion is interpreted as compulsion. The National Curriculum is compulsory in state schools in England and Wales and physical education is a foundation subject in that curriculum and is required at all Key Stages, i.e. throughout a child's compulsory schooling. Pupils are therefore required to do physical education. However, this compulsion does not really amount to coercion, which carries connotations of threats, being forced to act against one's will and the domination by one group of another. It is my contention that there is enough good within the subject, and enough good to be gained from learning the subject that it is right for physical education to be required.

Fernandez-Balboa also claims that physical education is reproductive. This means that it plays its part in replicating the social system and power relationship structure in which it is located. The maintenance of the status quo and the continuation of society have already been mentioned as a part of the structural functionalist view of society. The fact that physical education is part of an education system that strives to socialize its participants into 'useful' members of society lends considerable weight to this argument.

Physical education tends to produce young people who will replicate the values of their teachers, who in turn pass on the values of their society. It also reproduces the same sporting activities with each subsequent generation. There has been very little change in physical education curriculum content in the last fifty years (Kirk, 1992) in spite of introductions such as health-related exercise.

Summary

The claim that school sport and physical education can have negative outcomes is illustrated quite clearly in this commentary on the hidden curriculum. This should serve as a warning to those involved in curriculum design and delivery. However, it has also been demonstrated that the curriculum has much to offer that is of benefit. It appears then that there is a large amount of power resting in the hands of those involved in education and that care must be taken in the exercise of this power. From the wide-ranging interpretation of the affective domain in the critiques discussed, it seems that influence can be very broad indeed. This is confirmed by the extent to which sport and physical education pervade our lives and existence. As a major part of popular culture, as a socializing influence in the educational establishment, and as an educational tool in their own right, sport and physical education certainly form an institution with a power that has yet to be fully realized, and a vast potential for good.

5 From Theory into Practice
What Really Happens in Schools

This chapter will chart and discuss research into the real-life world of physical education in schools. What goes on in the gymnasium, or on the sports field or in the sports hall? I hope to indicate clearly what we currently know about teaching and about what the teaching and, crucially, the learning, of physical education achieves for the pupils who experience the school subject. There has been a series of easily identifiable phases in classroom research not only into physical education, but also into teaching in general, and these will be discussed, and instances of 'landmark' studies described, to obtain as full a picture as possible about what really happens in school physical education. Although much of the research referred to has been conducted in the United States, I have included studies from elsewhere, particularly Britain, where appropriate and relevant.

Early Research

The earliest investigations into teacher effectiveness were made in the 1920s and 1930s. Surveys to find out 'what makes an effective teacher' produced the answer that good teachers were warm, caring and organized. However, these surveys, in which the respondents were administrators, teachers and pupils merely established opinion and did not make any correlation with pupil learning or achievement. All one can say about the results of such research is that the types of teacher that are described are perhaps nicer people to be around and nicer people to be taught by than other types of teacher. Therefore, with a small leap of imagination, it might be possible to suggest that these warm, caring and organized teachers had a better chance of creating a more conducive learning environment than others. Another small step enables us to suggest that, because of this environment, more learning would have taken place. This may well be true, but from a scientific point of view this sequence of leaps of imagination and suggestions is far removed from a proven case consisting of a cause and effect relationship.

These surveys of opinions made use of Likert-type instruments which were being used at this time by psychologists. It is commonly known that research in physical education follows educational research, and that educational research invariably follows the direction taken by psychology. Here we also have an example of the current research methods leading the enquiries; Likert scales were popular, therefore they were used. This naturally determined the type of data generated, which in turn determined the type of findings made.

Correlation studies were another method of research common at this time. Within education these sought to link teacher characteristics to pupil outcomes. Not only were there found to be no common characteristics among teachers who achieved good pupil outcomes, but there were also no correlations noted between certain types of teacher characteristics and pupil outcomes. Although this did not provide empirical support for the view that good teachers were warm, caring and organized, it did not contradict it either. Therefore this view of what good teachers were like persisted – and to some extent still does to this day.

These lines of research continued into the late 1940s with researchers still trying to identify whether things such as social background or economic status had a bearing on teacher effectiveness. Failure to produce any consistent findings led to a decline in interest in this area. What made a good teacher, how children learned and what helped them to learn were still something of a mystery.

Teacher Behaviour

Researchers turned their attention to what teachers actually did in the classroom in attempts to identify good practice. This new idea, that teacher behaviours affected learning, began a line of enquiry which at last started to establish what made a good, or effective, teacher. This turning point also marked the change from surveys and correlation studies to descriptive and analytical studies located in the positivist research paradigm. Flanders (1960, 1970) can be credited with beginning this new era. His interaction analysis system (FIAS) was designed to be used in classrooms and to record what interactions teachers had with pupils. It was the first time that any judgement of teaching ability was based on observation of what was really going on in the classroom. Cheffers (1973) adapted the FIAS for use with non-verbal interactions, ideal for physical activity settings. This was the first of a plethora of systematic observation instruments designed to record the interactions and behaviours of teachers and pupils in a physical education setting. This is of course another example of the development of new methodologies leading the direction of research, but this time the instruments began to produce concrete, verifiable results.

At about the same time, Dunkin and Biddle (1974) were proposing a process–product theory. This assumed that teachers brought to lessons a certain profile of characteristics, called 'presage'. Similarly, pupils had a set of characteristics which, when added to the teaching environment, created a set of circumstances called the 'context'. The interaction that took place in the lesson, that is the lesson itself, was the process that produced the outcome known as the 'product'. Hopefully, the process was a learning experience that culminated in a change in behaviour known as learning. The *Beginning Teacher Evaluation Study* in California (Fisher et al., 1978) looked at mathematics and English lessons taught by newly qualified teachers. The project established that the amount of time pupils spent in academic learning time (ALT), or more specifically, 'on-task' was a determinant of how well they learned.

Physical education researchers changed direction and began to develop instruments for the observation of teaching and pupil behaviour in physical education settings. This change started a very productive line of research, which continued for fifteen to twenty years. ALT in physical education (ALT–PE) became accepted as a proxy variable for pupil learning, meaning that measurement of ALT–PE could be substituted for measurement of learning. The argument was that because pupils could learn more when they had more ALT–PE, the teachers that provided more ALT–PE were more effective teachers because their pupils would learn more. The logic was attractive but potentially flawed: several key components were missing from the chain. What if pupils were 'on-task' practising, but practising wrongly? To use the example of taking penalties in soccer, if the pupils were kicking the ball with the toe, instead of the instep, then the proper skill would not be being practised at all and therefore would not be learned. It is not just practice that makes perfect, but perfect practice that makes perfect. And what if the pupils were practising jump shots in basketball but not scoring any baskets? Would this assist learning? Obviously not. So, attractive as it was as a proxy variable for learning, ALT–PE needed certain other conditions to be met before it could be categorically stated that more ALT–PE led to more skill learning. The increasing use of observation instruments has provided the profession with a wealth of information about teacher and pupil behaviour that has eventually led to the situation nowadays where we can say with some certainty that, from a technical, behaviourist point of view, we know what behaviours are demonstrated by a good and effective teacher and that we thus know what it takes for a teacher to teach physical skills.

A short trip now brings us to the present day knowledge of performance pedagogy. This will set the scene for the departure from research located in the quantitative paradigm, to research located in the qualitative paradigm.

Much of the research into performance pedagogy was initiated by The Ohio State University research programme into physical education teacher effectiveness, led by Daryl Siedentop. Taking up the idea that ALT was important to good teaching practice, the Academic Learning Time–Physical Education (ALT–PE) instrument was developed (Siedentop, Tousignant and Parker, 1982). This enabled researchers to code and quantify teacher and pupil behaviours. Of all the instruments subsequently developed to measure similar variables (Darst, Zakrajsek and Mancini, 1989) the ALT–PE was, and probably remains, the most popular. But merely to describe what teachers did in class was not the sole purpose of this line of enquiry. Earlier work by Bloom (1980) had proposed that teacher behaviour variables were alterable. Therefore, the argument was that intervention strategies designed to improve the pattern of teacher behaviour could enable teachers to improve their performance and increase the learning of their pupils. But before this intervention could take place, the pattern of teacher behaviour had to be established and the efficacy of various intervention strategies had to be tested. Part of the impetus for this was a study by Phillips and Carlisle (1983) that found substantial differences in patterns of teacher behaviours between the most and least effective teachers. This combination of the identification of patterns of effective behaviours and less effective behaviours, and the belief that these behaviours were alterable, paved the way for a major research effort in physical education teaching.

Performance Pedagogy, The Ohio State University 'School' of Research and What Physical Education Teachers do in Lessons

The research summarized here is firmly located in the quantitative paradigm. The ability of teachers to produce physically skilled learners was the sole focus. There was a concentration on physical performance of both teachers, in terms of their teaching behaviours, and pupils, in terms of their learnt physical skills. If we relate this to the four domains of physical education (psychomotor, affective, cognitive and social), the affective, social and cognitive were virtually ignored and the psychomotor domain was given a privileged place in the research programme. I have therefore adopted the term 'performance pedagogy' to describe body of research produced from this background.

Working with a series of doctoral students, Daryl Siedentop, of The Ohio State University, produced a body of work that forms the foundation, and much of the structure, of what we know about teacher and learner behaviours. We will look here at some of the major findings of The Ohio State University school, as well as major contributions from other investigations. At least one factor clearly identifies this work as a relative departure from what had gone before; the work is firmly based on systematic observational analysis of real-life settings. The location of the observation settings was usually whole classes being taught curriculum physical education. So the data reflects what was going on in natural settings. Real classes were also used when teacher behaviour variables were manipulated to test whether interventions would improve performance.

Research has shown that teachers of physical education spent most of their time managing and organizing pupils, instructing pupils and monitoring performance and behaviour. Although results vary according to the research setting, roughly one third of lesson time is given to each of these activities (Smith, Kerr and Wang, 1993; Metzler, 1989). This finding alone has huge ramifications for the teaching of physical education. If pupils are being observed practising (monitored) for a third of the lesson time, then for two thirds of the time they are being organized or instructed. This means that their practice time could be limited to one third of lesson time. Fink and Siedentop (1989) found that there is more management and organization time at the beginning of the school year when teachers use time to establish rules and routines for their classes. Metzler (1989) found that instruction time was particularly high at the beginning of a unit of instruction and that pupil participation was higher towards the end. For example, when beginning to teach rugby, a teacher would spend considerable amounts of time on safety issues to ensure that a game of sorts – maybe a conditioned game such as tag rugby instead of the full contact game – could take place safely. Nearer the end of the unit, the teacher would be more interested in seeing the pupils demonstrate their skills in a game-type situation, and there would therefore be more pupil participation time than at the beginning.

In their critique of the studies on teacher effectiveness Rosenshine and Furst (1971) concluded that a number of factors were conducive to pupil learning. Four of these were dominant. First, there was pupil opportunity to learn – this is also known as academic learning time or time-on-task. Second, there was decreased criticism of pupils by the teacher. Knowing that efforts to work and practise will not be negatively viewed means a great deal to pupils in terms of encouragement. Third, the teacher should attempt to use structured comments to address mistakes and errors in the class's skill performance. Specific performance feedback is crucial here. And last, the use of direct, high order questions was best in guiding the pupils to evaluate and develop their own skills.

The use of performance feedback has already been briefly discussed. It must be accurate and so the teacher has to accurately diagnose errors in pupils' performance and know what advice to give to remedy those errors. The teacher therefore needs a high level of subject, or content, knowledge.

Put simply, effective teachers of physical education maximize the time that their pupils can spend practising their skills with a reasonable level of success, while at the same time minimizing the time spent on management and organization of the class. They are able to detect and correct errors in performance while at the same time creating a positive learning environment by avoiding negative comments to pupils. Having established what effective teachers do was the first step. Research then began into whether teaching behaviours could be altered, as Bloom (1980) claimed.

One of the most recent studies demonstrated that interventions can indeed cause a change in teaching behaviour. Meek and Smith (1998) used a single-subject, multiple baseline design to investigate changes in the teaching behaviour of one physical education student teacher. The behaviours targeted for improvement were performance feedback and motivation feedback. Performance feedback was defined as feedback based upon skill performance and aimed at improving that performance. Motivation feedback was defined as responses to pupils that are encouraging or reinforcing, (positive and negative). Both these behaviours were measured for three weeks by a coding instrument similar to the ALT–PE, the Physical Education

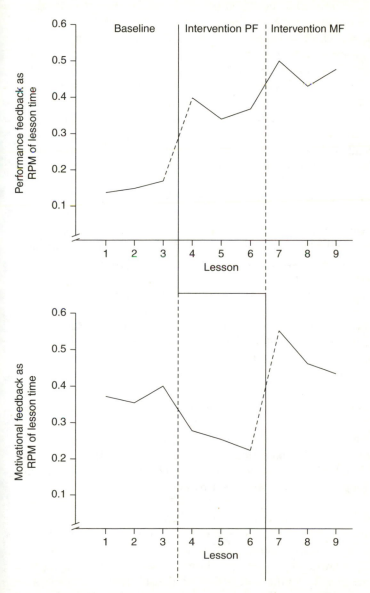

Figure 5.1 Rate per minute (RPM) of performance (PF) and motivation feedback (MF) for the subject during multiple baseline design

Teacher Assessment Instrument (PETAI) (Phillips, Carlisle, Steffen and Stroot, 1986), to obtain a baseline assessment of the amount of each behaviour that the student teacher used. The first intervention occurred after lesson three, when the student teacher was provided with a definition of performance feedback, the purpose of the intervention and information about the amount of performance feedback that he had used in the first three lessons. Lessons continued to be coded using the PETAI for a further three weeks but without any specific comments on the two targeted types of feedback. After the sixth lesson, the second intervention occurred, similar to the first in structure but concerned with motivation feedback. Last, the final three lessons were coded with the PETAI.

The results (Figure 5.1) clearly show that both types of feedback increased dramatically following the interventions. So teaching behaviours, and therefore teacher effectiveness, can be altered by strategies designed to do so. There are some notes of caution however. The study used only one subject, making it difficult to apply these results to other settings. But as Borg and Gall (1989) recognize, this type of method is particularly well suited to research on behaviour modification and was thus appropriate in this study. The longest time period that was monitored was that between the giving of information about performance feedback and the end of the study. We are presented with six weeks of data in which performance feedback shows an increase. It would be interesting to know whether this trend continued, or levelled out or eventually decreased. The three weeks in which the motivation feedback was tracked did in fact show a decrease in that behaviour. The authors suggest that the decrease might be as a result of the student teacher concentrating too much on performance feedback.

A similar study, using the same method, by Smith, Kerr and Meek (1993) was conducted with an experienced teacher. The first intervention, after four weeks, produced a rise in performance feedback. When the motivation feedback intervention was introduced performance feedback dropped off, and, after its initial increase, so did the motivation feedback (Figure 5.2).

Again it would be useful to know if these beneficial effects on teacher behaviour are maintained over time, and the authors do make the point that single subject designs do not allow the results to be generalized. These two studies prove only the existence of a possibility; that effective teacher behaviours can be enhanced by intervention. The best type of intervention and the long-term effects still need to be determined.

To summarize this section, research has shown us what makes good physical education teachers. We know what teachers and pupils do in class, and we know that effective teacher behaviours can be improved. All this research has concentrated on the psychomotor aspect of teaching and learning; on the physical skills that are so obviously the focus of physical education lessons. Of course this does not tell us what physical education means to its participants or what they feel about being part of physical

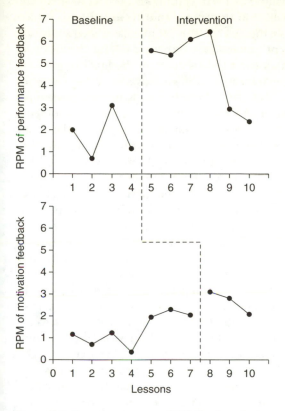

Figure 5.2 Rate per minute (RPM) of performance and motivation feedback for the subject during baseline and intervention phases

education lessons. It tells us what goes on in lessons, but it does not tell us how lessons happen. We still need to know the mechanics of lessons taking place and how different meanings and attitudes contribute to learning in all domains of physical education.

Attitudes and Meanings: How Lessons Happen and What Pupils and Teachers Feel About Physical Education

Literature from the field of sociology tells us how lessons happen and the types of interactions that go on in classes (Delamont, 1983). Teachers and pupils come to class with preconceived ideas of what will happen in the lesson, what shape it will take and what it will 'look like'. That is why we get the typical beginning of lesson scenario: 'Can we have a game today, Miss?', followed by the standard reply, 'If you behave yourselves and do some practices well we might have time for a game at the end'. The pupils and teacher in this case have different ideas about what they want from the lesson. But there are also similarities in what they want. They both want a lesson to happen, they both want to enjoy it and they both want to feel that they have done something worthwhile at the end. The encounter described shows the beginnings of a certain amount of negotiation that takes place in order for both parties to get something of what they want from the lesson.

This process has been formalized by sociologists as a process of interaction. Research into the 'new sociology of education' is no longer new but it has left a legacy of discussion and theory that has formed a sociological framework for much enlightening work. What happens in the classroom, and why it happens, are the two most crucial questions addressed. The interactive process in a classroom that allows a lesson to take place is a complicated one, which must be viewed from a number of perspectives to be understood. At the simplest level it is a combination of what characteristics pupils bring to school (Hammersley and Woods, 1984) and what characteristics teachers bring to school (Hargreaves and Woods, 1984). This combination is not a symmetrical arrangement because the teacher has power derived from various sources: from his status as an adult, from his traditional authority as a teacher, from his legal authority and from his expertise in the subject matter he is teaching (Hargreaves, 1975). On the other hand, the pupil is not without power to disrupt, to not participate, to be absent, to be a competent bystander (Tousignant, 1981) and so on.

The symbolic interactionist viewpoint defines the process by attaching meaning to actions and communications, verbal and non-verbal. This attachment of meanings is the crux of qualitative research as opposed to quantitative research. It is what brings descriptive research to life instead of making it merely a collection of data. The successful conclusion of the interaction process is contingent on certain stages being sequentially followed and achieved. First, teachers and pupils must share a common definition of the situation. Each must know, in broad terms, what the situation is expected to be. Each must know what the lesson should 'look like', and what the expectations are that surround the lesson. Obviously if the two parties have different definitions and expectations for the same situation (as in our example earlier), there is considerable opportunity for conflict. This is why it is so important from the institution's point of view to establish 'rules and routines' very early in the pupils' school careers (Fink and Siedentop, 1989). Second, individual differences in the definition of the situation, especially those that are highly incongruent, need to be negotiated and agreed if the interaction is to culminate in a satisfactory situation. As the negotiation proceeds the definitions held by the protagonists come closer together. The proximity of definitions will determine how well the third stage of consensus, will work.

This working relationship, although initially achieved by negotiation, needs to be supported by continual interpretation of each party's acts (Delamont, 1983), so that the definitions of the situation may be kept close. Close definitions allow high consensus, whereas divergent definitions cause discord in consensus and hence a problematic working relationship. Nevertheless, for a lesson to occur a consensus of sorts must exist, the quality of which is determined by the teacher and the pupils.

To apply this interpretive, theoretical framework to physical education is a fruitful path of enquiry. The interaction process was more closely analysed by Griffin (1984, 1985) in descriptions of participation patterns of middle-school pupils. Griffin identified types of participants and their strategies for coping and negotiating tasks within physical education lessons. As an example, boys in team sports assumed group identities such as 'machos', 'nice guys' and 'wimps' (Griffin, 1985). These labels characterized and defined their behaviour and their personas that were evident in lessons.

Pollard (1988) used an interpretive perspective to investigate and discuss non-specialist teachers' apprehension about teaching physical education in primary schools. He suggested that teachers were comfortable in their own classroom environments but were less happy in the open, less controlled circumstances of the physical education settings of the field, the gymnasium and the sports hall.

Other work by Martinek (1988, 1989) described how the perceptions and expectations held by pupils and teachers affect the two groups in terms of what was taught and what was learnt. Martinek (1988) found that pupils for whom the teacher had high expectations perceived that they were praised more than reprimanded. However, it was really the case that these pupils received more corrective behaviour feedback than any other response from the teacher. It was suggested that this misperception was caused because the pupils thought that praise was appropriate to them and so they expected to receive it as a result of a good performance.

Ennis (1990) reported on the curriculum in differing domains. She examined the ideological (philosophical and theoretical background), the formal (school curriculum interpretation and documentation), the perceived (what the teachers said they did), the experiential (what the pupils experienced in lessons) and the operational (what really took place in lessons) domains of the curriculum. Ennis found that, in most cases, the guiding influence of teaching in the schools was the ideological curriculum. However, when the ideology was not specified, other emphases became more explicit. So a pragmatic development, such as command style teaching rather than guided discovery, might occur in the operational domain if the direction of an umbrella philosophy were not available. In general though, the pupils confirmed the curriculum emphasis that was used by the teachers.

Pupil attitudes

In attempting to understand how lessons happen a knowledge of what the 'actors' bring to the situation is necessary. Attitudes, perceptions, expectations and beliefs of pupils and teachers will give information which can be used in interpreting interaction in the gymnasia and on the sports fields.

Attitude measurement and research has long been a topic of enquiry in physical education. However, it is only since the development of instruments to measure these traits (Edgington, 1968; Kenyon, 1968; and Martens, 1975) that a body of knowledge has been gathered that gives a fairly accurate picture of what pupils think of physical education and also of what factors are important in affecting those attitudes.

Most instruments to measure attitudes take the form of checklists, questionnaires or rating scales, all requiring a response from the pupil. One problem of data gathering by this method is a known tendency for the respondents to answer in a way that is most likely to bring approval. However, the responses of pupils are so similar in the majority of reports that there is evidence to believe that, in general, pupils answer truthfully.

A major influence on attitudes is pupil skill, in that those with higher skill levels tend to like physical education better than less able pupils (Carlisle et al., 1984). Although many pupils with low ability had good attitudes towards the subject, high ability and positive feelings are invariably interlinked. High ability performers also enjoyed the variety of activities, the opportunity to compete in what they were good at and the social aspects of working as a team. These experiences gave great enjoyment and contributed to self-esteem (Underwood, 1988). The one aspect of physical ability that did not appear to be associated with attitudes was physical fitness (Sherril, Holquin and Caywood, 1989).

Earl and Stennett (1987) found that boys generally had more positive attitudes than girls towards physical education. Within this broad finding, girls had preferences based on recreation, social and health factors, and enjoyment; whereas boys preferred risk activities, games and competition. These findings are supported by Dickinson and Sparkes (1988), who also found that girls had a preference for non-contact activities. Smoll and Schutz (1980) indicate that girls show more favourable attitudes towards the aesthetic subdomain than boys, but boys showed significantly more positive attitudes towards physical education as a medium for catharsis and the pursuit of thrills.

Better teachers encourage more positive attitudes (Aicinena, 1991). Aicinena's work elaborates on this point: if a teacher allows some input into classroom decision making, thus empowering the pupils while maintaining overall control, this will enhance attitudes. Pupils at all levels, both boys and girls, valued personal interactions with their teachers. Frequent and good quality reinforcement, feedback and attention were the most favoured interactions. Clark (1971) found that the physical education teacher was the second most popular figure in primary schools, the most popular being the pupils' own classroom teacher. Better teachers also learned names more quickly and allowed some socializing among the pupils.

Physical education benefits greatly from an overall positive view. A sample of British 11 and 12 year olds indicated that 94 per cent enjoyed physical education (Coe, 1984). In the USA, Rice (1988) found that 85 per cent of those surveyed enjoyed their physical education classes. There is also a perception of importance reported in some studies. In Dickinson and Sparkes's (1988) survey 52.9 per cent placed physical education third behind English and mathematics, in subject importance. When asked to name their favourite subject, the subject pupils named most often was physical education (Scott and West, 1990).

Pupils and parents hold similar views when it comes to deciding what is of value in physical education. Pupils in Canada value social contact, learning new skills, having fun and keeping fit (Earl and Stennett, 1987). Similarly, parents in the USA think that physical education is important for fitness, skill and social interaction (Stewart and Green, 1987). Parents did not value the cognitive and affective domains so much. Eighty-five per cent of parents felt physical education should be compulsory, and 75 per cent thought that it warranted credit, although there was less support for grades and written tests. A report by Pritchard (1988) in Britain indicated similar findings. Most of the sample valued the subject for the improvement of personal health and fitness and for the development of good sporting behaviour. Parents in the sample thought that moral and social training was important. Over 80 per cent strongly agreed that physical education should always be in the curriculum and that its essentially practical nature should be emphasized. Thus parents in both the USA and Britain value physical education with an emphasis on physical and social development, rather than the theoretical and cognitive aspects of movement.

In spite of all the favourable data presented so far, pupils' attitudes to physical education vary at some stages of schooling. McMillen (1992) found a decline in positive attitudes between the 4th and 6/7th grade. In Britain, Jones (1988) found a similar decline between the ages of 12 and 13 years. One explanation suggested that pupils at these ages are becoming more aware of alternative attractions besides school and home. This proliferation of choice inevitably dilutes the number who maintain an active interest in school physical education.

Teacher attitudes

Generally then, pupils bring a positive attitude to physical education lessons. They tend to enjoy what they do and they value the subject, as do parents. It can reasonably be suggested that pupils with these characteristics should be receptive to the teaching of the lesson content. However, it has been said that there is a mismatch between stated aims and pupils' beliefs about physical education (Physical Education Association of Great Britain and Northern Ireland, 1987; Underwood, 1983, 1988). The teachers' views of the subject illustrate this mismatch: two main avenues of research into teachers' perceptions of physical education have been aims, objectives and curriculum content; and occupational socialization into the profession. The former have been discussed earlier, but the latter now requires some attention to elaborate on 'what teachers bring to lessons'.

Occupational socialization discusses how various factors influence people entering the field of physical education, and how these factors are therefore responsible for their perceptions and actions as teachers (Lawson, 1986). Studies in this area provide detailed analysis of the process (Templin and Schemmp, 1989) and anecdotal descriptions of how teachers react to prolonged exposure to the role of the physical educator (Sikes, 1988). Even after brief exposure in the role, perceptions change. Arrighi and Young (1987) found that preservice and inservice teachers had strong consensual agreement on what factors were important to effective teaching: both groups identified learning time, management, knowledge of skills and safety. However a change that may be attributed to socialization (or confronting reality!) was from student teachers' concern with pupil learning, to inservice teachers' concern with self. Part of the reason for these changes in attitude may be the perceived low status of physical education in the hierarchy of school subjects. Hendry (1975) reports that pupils, physical education teachers, colleagues and administrators all viewed the subject as possessing little importance. Sparkes (1987) comments in a similar manner that physical education lacks prestige, wealth (in terms of salaries) and authority (in terms of career positions). In spite of the fact that physical education is a foundation subject in the National Curriculum there was a feeling of 'marginality', that is, it was seen as peripheral to the main goals and functioning of the organization.

Teachers' views of pupils have received some investigation. Hendry and Welsh (1981) revealed that teachers had different attitudes towards participants and non-participants. The most favourable attitudes were towards participants in extra-curricular sports, and competitive pupils were viewed as having many positive characteristics. Surprisingly, Placek (1983) found that student learning was not of much concern to the teachers. Teachers most frequently had concerns for student enjoyment, participation and misbehaviour. In this way Placek characterized physical education teachers as defining teaching situations in terms of keeping students 'busy, happy, and good' (1983: 49).

Ecology of physical education lessons

This interaction–negotiation–consensus model is only one way of interpreting the real-life world of how physical education lessons happen. Another interesting way, that more easily takes account of some affective aspects of physical education, is to treat the physical education classroom as a place of different, and in some cases competing, ecological systems. This emphasizes the naturalness of the lesson setting and allows for its changing nature as a living entity. An ecology is a group of natural organisms, environments and systems that work together and interact with each other to find and maintain a natural balance so that the whole system can survive and continue. Any disturbance to the delicate balance of the ecology from alien forces, e.g. an oil spill in a lake, can upset that balance with devastating consequences. Similarly, once an ecology of a class is established it resists change and influence from outside forces which could upset its balance. Just as with the lake and the oil however, external forces can cause disturbance if they are allowed to influence the classroom ecology.

This ecology model was first applied to the school situation by Doyle (1979). Tousignant (1981) and Tousignant and Siedentop (1983) then applied Doyle's concept of an ecological approach to classroom investigation in the physical education context. The ecological makeup of physical education classes is made up of three major task systems. Each system has a series of tasks that need to be accomplished for the system to be operable. There are the managerial task system, the instructional task system and the pupil social system.

The managerial system refers to what the teacher does to organize and manage the class to allow teaching to take place. So, getting the class changed, calling the register and organizing into teams or groups are tasks that fall into the managerial task system. Presenting information about the content of the lesson, instructing pupils in skills and giving subject based feedback are tasks that fall into the instructional task system. Both these systems are, to a large extent, in the teacher's control; they are what the teacher wants to do in the lesson. The teacher wants to manage the class in a way that allows them to instruct in the physical skills of the subject content. This is the teacher's agenda.

The third component of the ecology is the pupils' social system. Pupils usually come to physical education lessons with other things on their agenda besides taking part. We have already seen that physical education is held in quite high regard by pupils. For many it is one of their favourite subjects. Part of what makes it a favourite is the social nature of the subject, the ability of the pupils to socialize while taking part in lessons. They want to work with their friends and enjoy a social occasion. This is the pupils' agenda. Quite naturally, and unknowingly, pupils are creating and experiencing a situation that is said to promote social interchange, values and attitudes. They are indulging in a form of lesson interaction that will involve the development of affective outcomes.

How well the pupils do the instructional and managerial tasks is determined by how clear and explicit the instructions are and to what extent the teacher supervises the execution of the tasks. Tasks that have been clearly explained and are closely supervised are more likely to be completed properly than those tasks that are ambiguously explained and poorly monitored. In the latter case it is known that pupils sometimes modify the task to allow more social behaviour, and sometimes indulge in off-task behaviour. So the way the tasks are intially explained (known as the clarity and/or ambiguity) and the closeness of the monitoring have an effect on the ecology of the lesson.

Sometimes the pupils' social system might manifest itself as disruptive or inappropriate behaviour. When this happens, the managerial and instructional task systems of the teacher are challenged and a mechanism for control has to be implemented. This mechanism is called accountability. The whole of the ecological task system is driven by the way in which the teacher implements accountability. If the pupils are not held accountable for their performance, their effort or their behaviour, then the managerial and instructional tasks can be suspended and the pupil social system will become the paramount system. A teacher who imposes a restrictive and dominant managerial system by using high accountability will effectively suspend the pupil social system altogether. In most cases the interactions of the three systems with each other result in a balance of interests held together by a web of elastic tensions, allowing change throughout the course of a lesson but never reaching a breaking point that would nullify what all the participants, teacher and pupils alike, really want to happen: an effective and enjoyable physical education lesson.

In many ways this is like the interaction–negotiation–consensus model of lesson interpretation. The major difference is that the ecology model actively recognizes that there are other possible outcomes from physical education lessons besides physical and cognitive elements. The attraction of the ecology model is that it encourages teachers to consider affective outcomes even if they do not think them to be important. It illustrates that affective outcomes are part of physical education, albeit from the pupils' perspective. As a theoretical model of lesson implementation the ecology of physical education has much to recommend it.

Perceptions of Lesson Content in Physical Education

The interaction between teaching and learning has become a fruitful ground for investigation in physical education as studies at the micro-level become more popular. This, after all, is the critical moment in the teaching–learning continuum when learning happens. Research into this interaction is important because it allows us to know what is really happening, instead of having a preconceived idea of what should be happening. The possibility that perception might not match reality is not so unlikely.

What teachers teach

Placek (1983) found that teachers did not consider pupil learning to be a real consideration in effective teaching. If this finding is taken at face value, it raises a new set of questions. If pupils do not learn what we teach, why teach it? What do pupils learn, or think they learn, in physical education? Are pupils being taught the covert values of the hidden curriculum – as Fernandez-Balboa (1993) so eloquently argues – as opposed to, or in addition to, the stated curriculum aims?

Erikson (1982) has argued that the hidden curriculum has been extensively researched and that what is needed now is investigation into the pedagogical encounter. By this he means that the teaching and learning interaction, the 'pedagogical moment', could benefit from further investigation that would open our understanding of it, much as the hidden curriculum has been made overt by investigation and elaboration.

It is implied by these issues that pupils do not necessarily learn what teachers say they teach. If teachers were effective at communicating to pupils what they were teaching, there would be no discrepancies between teachers' and pupils' perceptions of lesson content. Beglin (1968) suggested that where there are discrepancies some conflict may result. It seems to be stating the obvious to say that if pupils and teachers hold different perceptions of the teaching/learning process, then effective education will prove more difficult than if those perceptions are the same.

Underwood (1983) investigated the stated purposes of physical education. He found that the extent to which teachers communicated their objectives to children is not known. He further suggested that the implementation of any curriculum plan can only take place during the actual lesson and that research into lesson transaction is sparse. Underwood concluded by saying that a lack of congruence between teachers' and pupils' perceptions indicated the need for more precise planning and research. Ennis's work (1985) supports this view. In a comparison of the stated purposes of physical education across four domains (formal, perceived, operational and experiential), Ennis found considerable discrepancies. Other studies by Wang (1977), Underwood (1988) and Lambdin and Steinhardt (1992) report similar mismatches between perceptions of content and purpose.

The report by the Physical Education Association of Great Britain and Northern Ireland (PEA) contained some disturbing quotations from teachers of the subject in primary schools: 'Few pupils are aware of the process'; 'Pupils are taught but whether they understand is debatable', 'Most children enjoy their PE but apart from those who are trained to think there is not much understanding' (1987: 13). These quotations indicate the reason for the report, i.e., concern for the way physical education was being taught in England and Wales.

Since the PEA report, a National Curriculum has been established for schools in England and Wales (Department of Education and Science, 1992 and Department for Education, 1995) and physical education has been included as a foundation subject in it. Specific subject requirements have been published and nearly half of these requirements are non-physical. Teachers must now take account of these requirements when designing their school-specific curricula and individual lessons. The differing requirements certainly raise again the twin concepts of education through the physical, and/or education of the physical. The variety of requirements suggests that physical education may fulfil a role within the school curriculum over and above the merely physical.

Lesson emphasis

The results of the previously mentioned studies and the requirements of the National Curriculum appear to be inconsistent. A study by Laker (1995b) investigated these inconsistencies and made some interesting findings. Teachers and pupils were interviewed separately after lessons had been taught to determine whether their perceptions of lesson content differed. The domains of the physical education curriculum selected to allow organization of the data from this study were: psychomotor (or physical); affective, cognitive and social.

Dominance of psychomotor

The investigation revealed that the teachers placed the majority of their emphasis on the purely psychomotor components of their lessons. Some emphasis was placed on both the affective and cognitive domains. Very little, if any, emphasis was placed on the social characteristics of physical education.

Some statements regarding the psychomotor domain were very general, such as: 'to improve the quality', and 'helping them to refine their movements'. This type of statement was not common however; most physical statements tended to be very specific, such as 'a simple tuck, pike, straddle', and 'using the flat of the stick to stop the ball'. These specific statements seemed to be a reflection of the teachers' concern with, and application of, behavioural objectives, as stated in their lesson plans. The importance that teachers placed on specific physical objectives can be seen by the fact that one volleyball teacher repeated three times, 'how to set, how to spike', during the interview. All teachers perceived that all their lessons had a majority of psychomotor elements. Approximately 60 per cent of teachers' statements were assigned to the psychomotor domain.

The affective domain was perceived by the teachers as being the second most important aspect of their lessons. About 20 per cent of their statements were assigned to this domain. All the teachers made at least one statement concerning the affective. These statements usually related to working together, working as a team, cooperation and communication. Statements ranged from simple, 'they've learned to cooperate' to complex, 'to be sympathetic with their passes, to think about their partner and to think about the consequences of their actions'.

The cognitive domain received the third largest number of statements (just under 20 per cent), although the number was small when compared to the huge number of psychomotor statements. Most cognitive comments were about understanding principles and tactics. In a soccer lesson, 'a greater tactical awareness of what they should be doing off the ball' was encouraged. Rules and concepts of sports and skills received some attention. A basketball lesson produced the question, 'what happens if someone is fouled in the act of shooting?' Lastly, there was some awareness of safety factors. Trampoline, weight-training and gymnastics lessons were the main sources for statements such as, 'also the safety point of view, getting out the equipment, checking it's OK, so that was another thing I was trying to get over to them'. All lessons had elements of the cognitive, but it was usually very minimal, and in some cases just one comment.

The social domain received comments from only two of the sixteen lessons. It appeared that the pupils' social task structure was not a factor in the teachers' perceptions of their lessons. One teacher said that 'anything that reinforces the social side of sport is good'. Another commented that 'they go with their friends anyway, people they will talk to and get on with'.

The perceptions of the pupils were that the psychomotor domain was dominant, and the cognitive and affective domians received little attention. Only one pupil made a comment about the social domain.

Comments from the pupils regarding the physical side of lessons were usually simplistic and limited to one or two aspects of the lesson, 'we were trying to work on a dance routine to fit the music', and 'to pass the ball in different ways'. A few pupils were able to identify more physical skills that they had been taught. After a hockey lesson a pupil described it as, 'improving our skills, passing with the stick, control and stopping it, how to back pass, run with the ball, and the speed to push it'. Although this pupil had been very aware of the physical, he made no comment on any other domain. Some only remembered parts of lessons, 'we did a lot of warm-up, stretching our muscles'. All the pupils made some comment on the psychomotor domain, but only half made any comments about the other domains. Approximately 65 per cent of pupils' statments were assigned to the psychomotor domain.

The few statements that were assigned to the affective domain identified cooperation, behaviour and effort in performance as the only characteristics worthy of mention. Such statements were small in number and content (about 15 per cent of all student statements). Some were simple and merely highlighted 'working as a team' and 'cooperation'. 'To be sensible and not stupid' and 'pay attention, not muck around' were a couple of the few that commented on behaviour. Another characteristic, 'giving 100 per cent all the time', and 'trying our best' was the third identified factor of the affective domain. Pupils did not recognize any affective factors apart from the limited selection above.

The cognitive domain was perceived as slightly more important than the affective (20 per cent), but as previously mentioned, this was minimal when compared to the psychomotor domain. Tactical awareness accounted for some of these statements, which came mostly from lessons on team games. A rugby lesson provided the statement, 'looking for the opposition to see where they are', and a soccer lesson provided, 'looking for space all the time to pass the ball into'. Another type of comment concerned knowledge necessary to perform a skill. This was notable in the weight-training lessons: examples were, 'How to tighten the weights and get the right weight', and 'same with the rowing machines and stepping machines he taught us how to use as well'. These statements are to do with knowledge acquisition. There were a few additional comments about health and fitness, and safety, but these were very much in the minority.

The only statement assigned to the social domain was, 'There were a lot of people talking to their friends'. It would seem that the pupils, like the teachers, did not mention any emphasis on the social interactions of physical education lessons. Perhaps the agenda of the pupil social task system is a hidden one. Although the teachers considered that it had some minimal sigificance, the pupils were unwilling to mention it.

Similarity of pupil and teacher perceptions

When comparing pupils' and teachers' perceptions of lesson content, it was apparent that there was a pattern of general agreement in the priority placed on the four domains. This is supported by the Ennis study (1990) where the perceived curriculum of the teachers and the experiential curriculum of the pupils were remarkably consistent.

This agreement was particularly strong in terms of the psychomotor domain which the pupils identified almost to the exclusion of the other domains. Pupils had very little ability to identify the teacher-stated non-physical content of physical education lessons. This was probably due to the fact that the physical was what the pupils actually did and practised in the lessons. In comparing perceptions of the psychomotor domain (and others), it was evident that teachers had more complex, and numerous, perceptions than did the pupils. The pupils' experience of the lessons was simply that, experiential, and it was a physical experience, not affective, cognitive or social.

Unless other content was articulated to the pupils there was no reason for them to be aware of it. Interestingly, in none of the lessons observed did the teacher categorically state what he was teaching. Instructions to the pupils were usually clear and concise, but the teacher never said, for example, 'Today, I will teach you . . .'. So the pupils' perceptions were based solely on implication and what they physically did in the lessons.

The differences in perceptions of non-physical content could better be described as lack of realization of non-physical content on the part of the pupils. Teachers identified, to some degree, items from the affective, cognitive and social domains. Pupils mentioned a few factors but hardly perceived any importance in those domains. However, within the affective domain pupils did identify cooperation, effort and behaviour as the factors that were promoted. These three factors are emphasized throughout the schooling process (Karabel and Halsey, 1977; Inglis, 1985). It seems that, in this domain, the pupils reported what the teachers expected of them. They were expected to cooperate with each other in activities, especially team games, they were expected to behave well and they were expected to make their best efforts in lessons. This shows that physical education was playing its part in promoting these values to students in an implicit form, because these factors were rarely, if ever, mentioned in the lessons observed.

The teachers viewed the cognitive domain as consisting mainly of tactical awareness, rules and safety. The pupils viewed only the tactical awareness factor as important. An explanation for this could be that the pupils realized that tactical ability allowed them to perform better in the activities, and that rules and safety merely provided the framework that allowed the activity to take place and were therefore secondary in importance and so not worthy of comment. The pupils' perception of tactical awareness was evident only in lessons on team games, as would be expected.

The social domain was not generally perceived by either pupils or teachers. Perhaps the social interaction that occurs in lessons, which are necessarily social settings, is considered such an accepted part of school life (Hammersley and Woods, 1984; Hargreaves and Woods, 1984), that participants were unaware of it or just took it for granted. Social interaction was observed in all lessons viewed but respondents did not consider it a domain for comment in interview.

Complexity of teachers' views

As one would expect, in all domain areas the teachers had more complex, numerous and complete perceptions than did the pupils. This may be accounted for by the teachers' 'ownership' of the lessons. Within the requirements of the National Curriculum the teachers had planned the units of work, and the lessons within those units. They had given thought to what the lesson would be like, what equipment would be needed and all the attendant considerations that physical education teachers must take into account before a lesson can be taught. The teachers had also established objectives for their lessons which they then reported in the interviews. This background of thought and preparation contrasts with the mere participation of the pupils.

The teachers' views of domain emphasis in physical education could have been the result of their training, work experience and teaching within a particular curriculum model, all in physical education. The pupils' views of domain emphasis were partly a result of their experiences of school life in general and partly of their experiences of physical education in school. The latter factor is in the complete control of the physical education teachers. In this regard the teachers are one of the prime determinants of pupils' views of physical education. The pupils viewed as important what the teachers portrayed as important (although not to the same degree) thus generating similarity of perception.

From the data collected in this study, it does not appear that the non-physical outcomes claimed for physical education are perceived as very important by pupils or teachers. In the few cases where they were commented on, they were usually linked to specific types of lesson content (e.g. self-expression and interpretation were linked to educational dance and gymnastics). The idea that non-physical outcomes may be achieved as a by-product of physical education could indeed be the case. As one teacher commented, 'I guess it's implied more, brought out by situations'.

The pupils' voice

Another source of much information about what really goes on in physical education lessons, or at least what pupils think goes on, is the 1995 issue of the *Journal of Teaching in Physical Education*. This described studies in the USA intended to find out what the various components of physical education meant to the pupils who experienced it.

The elementary school children in Dyson's (1995) study had views of what they had learned in physical education that were very similar to those of their teachers. The children thought that they had learned to cooperate with others, challenge themselves, take risks, have fun and learn new motor skills. In addition, Dyson notes that the pupils appeared to share many of their teachers' views on competition, cooperation and communication. This matches the findings from Laker (1995b), that teachers and pupils had similar perceptions of the content of their physical education classes. As suggested there, the reason is probably that the teachers are the ones who control what the pupils experience in their lessons.

Not all pupils have fun in physical education. This is particularly true for those who have lower levels of psychomotor ability. To have one's deficiencies permanently 'on display' can be very troubling and it should come as no surprise that these pupils do not like physical education and sports as much as more able pupils. Portman (1995) found that low skilled pupils enjoyed their physical education more when they were asked to do activities and skills that they were successful at. Either they could already perform the skill and were therefore operating in a comfortable 'safe zone', or they achieved immediate success when trying the new skill for the first time. The ideal class for these children would be one where they repeated activities that they could already do, or where they did activities that were easy enough for them to be successful. We find our notion of progression as a desirable quality of physical education being challenged. Educators naturally want children to learn and that implies that there should be some progression. However, if we redefine what we want children to learn for each category of pupil, we can accommodate different skill levels far more easily. For example, highly skilled children who enjoy being stretched and adapt easily to new skills clearly benefit from a traditional, progressive programme. On the other hand, pupils for whom physical education provokes trepidation derive little or no benefit from such a programme. Perhaps we should reconsider learning in terms of the attitudes and personal and social characteristics so often stated as goals for physical education, instead of merely the psychomotor development which usually receives the most attention.

Summary

It can be deduced from the foregoing that if physical education really educates through the physical, the process must necessarily be of a more covert nature than the literature suggests. If this is happening the teachers are not very aware of it, and the pupils even less so. Perhaps the hidden curriculum is so successfully hidden that its implementation is totally subliminal.

We are very close to knowing fully about what happens in school physical education lessons and those areas where we have less knowledge, such as the hidden curriculum and the affective domain, are currently being researched. This 'other side' of physical education is one of the final components in our complete understanding. However, now that we believe we know what really happens in physical education lessons, the profession is presented with a fresh set of challenges. Now that we have this knowledge, let us use it for the benefit of the individuals and society as a whole. There is an increasing call to educate children through the subjects, as well as educating them in the subjects. Physical education has been shown to be an ideal subject to take on this challenge and to help children to grow and develop into fully educated adults, who then play a full role in enhancing their lives and the lives of others in their communities.

6 Responsibility, Personal, Social and Moral Education, and Citizenship

Is This Physical Education for the New Millennium?

Should the school subject of physical education attempt to encourage pupils to be responsible for themselves, for their actions and for others? Additionally, should physical education take upon itself a responsibility to address issues of personal development, social education and the inculcation of moral values that society suggests are desirable in order for people to be socially functional and acceptable? And lastly, can and should physical education be concerned with the business of producing school leavers who are educated in citizenship, who are able to be rational and politically literate citizens, and who realize what the idea of citizenship means for a young person in society today?

Responsibility, for oneself, for one's actions and for others, is a thread that runs through the earlier historical account of the subject's evolution. Responsibility to the group for survival, responsibility to the state and to society both in citizenship and military terms, and corporate and individual responsibility in teams and independent sporting endeavours have all received considerable attention at varying times throughout the development of the subject. Education in Renaissance times was partly concerned with equipping people to take a place in polite, cultured society. To this end, they received social and personal education. It has been shown quite clearly that Greek and Roman education had as one of its aims the education of people as citizens of the state. So the historical precedent was set centuries ago. Whether the modern subject embraces them or not, physical education has a long history of contribution to these areas. This chapter examines this potential in greater detail and looks at the curriculum models and research that inform our discussions of physical education as a vehicle for developing responsible, and personally, socially and morally educated citizens.

Social Learning Theory

The concept of achieving these types of aims by using physical education is based upon two theories of learning. First is social learning theory (Bandura, 1977): in this theory children, or indeed any learners, observe the way socially acceptable behaviour is rewarded. They then adopt and demonstrate that behaviour in order to gain similar rewards. An example would be the mimicking of a teacher's or parent's actions. This is why certain types of teaching strategies such as modelling, discussed later, are so important. Teachers cannot escape the fact that they are role models, and social learning theory says that role models are extremely important in the formation of socially acceptable behaviour.

Structural-Development Theory

Second, there is structural-development theory (Haan, 1991). This describes a cognitive process that requires the individual to be able to interact with others, thus developing a learning structure based on changing patterns of behaviour in response to the actions and reactions of others and the environment. This is similar to the classroom interaction and negotiation process described in the ecology of physical education.

Put simply, whereas social learning theory requires learners to copy, structural-development theory requires learners to respond to others and their environment. How teachers and coaches use these theories in their teaching and coaching will determine what strategies they use to achieve the affective outcomes that are the subject of this chapter. For example, a teacher using social learning as a theoretical background might use teacher modelling and a reward system to enhance self-responsibility amongst her pupils. A teacher basing his teaching in structural-development theory could use small periods of time set aside during lessons for pupils to solve problems and reflect on the nature of the task. It can clearly be seen that the former lends itself more easily to being teacher-led, whereas the latter offers more possibilities for learner-led, or learner-centred, opportunities. What the teacher chooses will be determined by a number of factors, not least of which is what the teacher wants the learners to acquire from any lesson or set of lessons.

Responsibility

When discussing responsibility and physical education, one cannot approach the topic without a consideration and critique of the work of Don Hellison and Jim Stiehl in the USA.

Hellison has worked with youth 'at risk' in urban locations for many years. His work has rarely been tested empirically, but his response to this criticism is that our true, conscious experiences are valid data and that the truth is what we experience. Although this may not impress the positivist scientific community, it represents a line of qualitative reasoning which, as Hellison says, 'only takes one case to prove a possibility' (Hellison, 1983). The programme provides a framework for practical applications in physical activity settings, usually school-based.

Hellison (1983, 1985) asks the question, 'What is worth doing?' The response is that what is worth doing is what is of value. In relation to his particular concern for 'at risk' youth, Hellison points out that there are problems of alienation, displacement, rootlessess, drugs, despair, isolation and confusion. Hellison is talking about American society, but it would be foolish to deny that problems similar in nature, if not in stature, exist in British society. Having acknowledged the problems facing youth, and those involved in the education of youth, Hellison translates the characteristics needed to overcome these problems into needs such as the need for self-control, the ability to make responsible choices and the leading of a stable life. These needs, Hellison argues, can be met by a physical education curriculum based on what he calls levels of responsibility. His original levels of responsibility are detailed below, followed by a review of the more recently evolved levels (Hellison, 1996) and a demonstration of how they match and fit with Stiehl's three domains of responsibility.

Stiehl's work originates in similar concerns about the nature of physical education and the fact that its relevance to the lives of many children is questionable at best, and counterproductive and alienating at worst. The changing of games (Morris and Stiehl, 1998) to make them more appropriate to the needs of children and an exploration of the process of 'becoming responsible' (Stiehl, 1993) have formed the basis of Stiehl's work.

Hellison's levels of responsibility

There are five original levels of responsibility in Hellison's model through which a pupil can progress. Level 0, the first level, is lack of responsibility and is therefore called irresponsibility. At this point the pupils are unmotivated and undisciplined; they blame others for mistakes, will not take responsibility for their actions and hinder the efforts of others. These pupils lack direction and can see no value in physical activity, let alone school physical education. They would rather 'hang out' than take part, and they will mock those that do take part. Not all pupils begin at level 0 and some pupils will never visit this level.

Hellison points out that throughout their school careers, school pupils may operate at different levels on different occasions. Movement between levels and within levels is not necessarily a sequential, logical process. Pupils will start at different levels and progress at different rates, sometimes up the levels and sometimes down the levels. The aim of the programme, and therefore the aim of the teachers using the programme, is to empower the pupils to reach the highest level of responsibility they can.

The first step in the right direction for pupils at level 0 is a move to level 1. This level is that of self-control: here, pupils do not interfere with others and prevent their participation. Authority is starting to be transferred to the individual as opposed to originating with the teacher. Participation is not a criterion for the demonstration of level 1 characteristics, so pupils may or may not choose to take part fully in the lessons.

The possibility of non-participation is addressed in the next level; involvement in the physical activity of the lesson is a necessary component for level 2 behaviour to be recognized. Involvement in the activity of a lesson may seem a strange requirement to many teachers, who might expect pupils to take part anyway. But the context must be remembered here: Hellison has constructed his programme in response to the needs of disaffected youngsters. For some of this group, just being a productive part of a lesson is a major achievement.

Level 3 allows and encourages children to assume some self-responsibility. They begin to make their own choices based on knowledge of the consequences. (The National Curriculum contains an element of this, as pupils are expected to 'plan, perform and evaluate' their physical education activities.) Hellison's model expects children to reflect, plan, work and play within an appropriate framework. For pupils to take responsibility for their own lives in the changing world is the aim. This level marks the culmination of concern with self, self-control, involvement of self and self-responsibility. Beyond this, pupils are expected to have some concern for others.

This is elaborated in level 4, the final level, where caring for others is a key component. The giving of support, caring, help and cooperation are expected from children who are at this level of responsibility. There is an assumption expressed in the hierarchical arrangement of levels, that pupils have to be aware of their own needs and be able to cater for them before they can move on and start caring and reaching out to others.

It is at this final point that Hellison's model begins to approach the notion of citizenship. This is discussed in more detail later, but simply put, the idea of citizenship carries within it the concept of responsibility for oneself and for others. One argument suggests that the rights that one expects to have, e.g. the right to a peaceful existence, the right to justice and so on, are only available if one accepts that one has some responsibilities to maintain and apply those rights to others. But another point of view says that rights should be applied whether one is responsible or not.

The most recent version of Hellison's model of teaching personal and social responsibility (TPSR) also has five levels, but there are also smaller stages within the levels, for ease of interpretation and implementation. (For detailed explanations of Hellison's TPSR, see Hellison, 1996.) The levels are presented hierarchically to aid the notion of progression through the teaching and learning process. There are many similarities to the original model but there are also some crucial differences.

Hellison uses his old levels as goals in an attempt to present progress as a positive movement, instead of it having negative connotations of moving away from undesirable behaviours. He still accepts that many children and young adults involved in his programme will come to the programme operating at a level of irresponsibility, i.e. level 0. The later version imme-diately establishes level 1, respect, as goal 1, thus beginning the programme with the attainment of a positive trait, rather than the demonstration of a negative one. If the idea is presented sympathetically, pupils should aspire to beginning in a positive manner. The first goal now involves being able to use self-control in respecting others' rights, including the right to a peaceful and unthreatened existence. Hellison also includes the right to peaceful conflict resolution.

This progress through the programme then follows the pattern: attain a level, adopt the next level as a goal, and so on. There are also some semantic differences between the earlier model and the updated model which deserve exploration.

The second goal, of participation and effort, equates with the old level 2 of involvement. However, pupils are encouraged to acquire a personal definition of success. So, not only is involvement important, but success also receives some attention. This recognizes that pupils need success to continue participation but that success in conventional terms is not always appropriate to all pupils. Merely taking part might be a success for some, whereas not getting into conflict might be a success for others and achieving practical goals might mean success to another group. Generally accepted measures of success have to be suspended. To be measured against one's peers in this context is not appropriate and it may not be appropriate even to be measured against a task.

The old level 3, self-responsibility, becomes the goal of self-direction. The difference in title is subtle but it does demonstrate a different emphasis; instead of merely being responsible for their actions, the pupils are expected to be able to direct their actions in terms of physical activity. This implies some knowledge base that allows rational choices and decisions. Children who achieve this goal are now more able to work independently and be aware of how choices made now affect their actions and choices later on.

Sensitivity and responsiveness to the well-being of others replaces 'caring' as the new goal 4. Although concern for others and contributing to the community of learners are needed, so too is an increased range of inter-personal skills as well as an altruistic desire to help others. Nevertheless, the old level 4 and the new goal 4 are essentially the same.

Another major difference between Hellison's two models is the intro-duction of a new ultimate goal – goal 5 – in his latest model. Here participants are encouraged to take their new social and interpersonal skills beyond the classroom and into the community. This is extremely impor-tant in contributing towards the promotion of citizenship. After all, what is the point of developing responsible and caring young people if they only demonstrate such traits in the gymnasium, in the sports hall or on the sports field? Community responsibility is not limited to this level. Participants at level 3, self-responsibility, and level 4, concern for others, could also be expected to take those traits into community and public settings. The goal of Hellison's work can be seen to be the ability to care for oneself and others, at times, in any and all situations.

Applicability

As mentioned earlier, there has been a concern expressed by critics that traits demonstrated in physical education lessons may not transfer to situations outside the school setting, or even outside the physical education setting. Recent evidence (Sharpe, Brown and Crider, 1995; Mercier, 1992) indicates that there can be a transference of such 'prosocial' behaviours from the physical education setting to the whole-school setting. Hellison has obviously taken account of this evidence in his later model and has taken the idea a step further in suggesting and expecting that these behaviours be used at home, in the street and in the community.

To a large degree, the argument that physical education contributes to overall personal and social development has already been won. It is known that this achievement can carry over into benefits for the community and society, and this has huge ramifications for the subject, its place and importance in the curriculum, and the emphasis placed on its teaching in school.

Stiehl's model of responsibility

Stiehl recognizes this point when he talks about responsibility for the environment as a final stage in the development of responsibility. Although his framework is not developmental, it is value-based and eclectic. The key to his discussion is the increasing awareness that physical education does not exist in a vacuum. Schooling and physical education exist in, and because of, a wider context that incorporates cultural and societal ideas about what is important. It is the more altruistic of these values that Stiehl espouses in his work. It is accepted, at least in the western world, that schooling must have a contribution to make in developing and improving the quality of existence. As Stiehl says, what could be is probably more important than what is. Responsibilty means taking care of ourselves, others and our surroundings. This is categorized by Stiehl into personal, social and environmental responsibility, creating a model of responsibility that incorporates both self-interest and altruism. If the starting point is the idea of being responsible for oneself, it is clear that responsibility cannot be imposed from the outside. Rather, individuals progress through the increasingly altruistic stages of responsibility as they develop into rational and caring adults.

Personal responsibility

Personal responsibility includes a sense of self-worth. Because one is worth something as an individual, one must be accountable for one's actions and responsible to oneself for the consequences. When the conse-. quences of one's actions affect other people, social responsibility becomes a consideration.

Social responsibility

Caring for, honouring and respecting others and their worth is a basic requirement for the improvement of the human condition. If teachers want to 'improve' the children in their charge, they need to treat them with care and respect. This uses the concept of a role model in its finest way: if care and respect are offered to school children it is more likely that they will replicate those traits in their own behaviour. Demeaning children and 'putting them down' have no place in educating responsible citizens. Indeed, they have no place in education as a whole.

Environmental responsibility

Environmental responsibility concerns the physical world. Respect for prop-erty, for one's surroundings or for sports hall equipment are important but they pale into insignificance when compared to global responsibility for the physical community, the social community and the world. Environmental responsibility is not solely the province of individuals; it must also be the job of institutions, global corporations and nations. But these are all made up of individuals who have been educated in schools. Schools therefore have a chance to make a difference.

There are very obvious similarities between comparing the models presented so far. All three are hierarchical, but not necessarily develop-mental. There are domains, levels or goals that represent improved cate-gories of social behaviour. There is an implication of progress, although it is possible to exhibit behaviours and characteristics from different levels and domains at the same time. However, it is clearly not expected that children stay at a low level of behaviour without being encouraged to progress to a higher level. Hellison's later model has naturally evolved from his original idea. His later model concentrates more on positive and pro-active concepts and less on the absence of negative and antisocial characteristics, but adding an ultimate goal of applying responsibility outside school, which is extremely significant for physical education. This extra-mural application is mirrored by Stiehl's environmental respon-sibility. Hellison's first three levels and the zero level (in the original model) and first three goals (in the later model) roughly equate to Stiehl's first arena of responsibility, that is personal responsibility, while Hellison's fourth stage in both models equates to Stiehl's arena of social responsi-bility. The important thing about these conceptualizations of a physical education curriculum for developing personal and social responsibility is that they aspire to contributing to individuals' behaviour in contexts far removed from school.

This aspiration is part of a realization that education does not exist in isolation. The interconnectedness of differing forces and institutions in society offers a myriad of potentials for all its contributory elements. The recent trend in political economics of attributing economic trends to global forces indicates that we do indeed live in a 'global village'. This is also true in an educational context. Increasingly easy communication, both physical, though more accessible travel, and data-based, through cyber-technology, make the transmission of information and ideas around the world no more difficult than talking to the next door neighbour. This means that people are being educated now who will have a responsibility for what the world is like in the next century and beyond. More importantly, people are being educated now and formed by teachers into what *they* will be like in the next century. Hellison, Stiehl and others, myself included, feel that this is sufficient reason to make a conscious effort to include concepts of responsibility, respect and citizenship, amongst others, in today's physical education. Part of education for the next century clearly rests in personal, social and moral education and thus in the contribution that physical education can make to this area.

Personal, Social and Moral Education

The range of what is meant by personal, social and moral education (PSME), its different incarnations and its location in the school curriculum have been very diverse in recent times. However, there is now a complete recognition of its value and, as personal, social and health education (PSHE) it will become compulsory in all state schools. Nevertheless, even what is meant by the various terms has been open to many interpretations. With this in mind the term 'personal, social and moral education' has here been used as an intact term to discuss those aspects of education, and particularly physical education, that are concerned with the growth of the individual and the development of ethical and moral reasoning capabilities in that individual. The health aspects of PSHE will be discussed later.

The idea that schools develop people as well as educating them is part of the rationale for PSME. This is in recognition of the fact that humans are not unidimensional; there are many facets to us. We have intellectual selves, moral selves, social selves and physical selves, to name only a few. The introduction of PSME into schools recognizes this fact and seeks to educate the personal, social and moral self, alongside the others selves touched by schools. PSME appears in different forms. In some schools it is a timetabled subject. Others include it in the pastoral system. Yet others cover PSME in religious education, but all schools now have some form of PSME.

Many of the aspects of personal development through sport, physical activity and physical education have been alluded to in earlier chapters. Blake (1996) claims that the school curriculum offers a multiplicity of opportunities for the development of personal characteristics desirable for all individuals in society. Physical education in particular offers an interactive environment which includes skill acquisition, challenge and social exchange. Perhaps the key to the contribution that schooling, and especially physical education, can make in the area of personal development is the social nature of the experience. Children must learn to be with others, because of the nature of the environment. They therefore acquire a range of personal and social skills, almost by default, that enables them to cope with the situations in the school environment. What these skills actually are will depend on a large number of variables such as the way the pastoral system of the school is structured, the ethos of the staff, the emphasis of the physical education programme, and not least, the background of each individual child.

Laker (1996) provides a review of some relevant literature, detailing what characteristics various scholars have suggested might be achieved through physical education. These do not only involve cooperative characteristics, which might easily be recognized in a socially interactive context, but also individual traits that might develop as a result of participation in physical education. It must be acknowledged that participation in sport and physical activity has the potential for detrimental, as well as desirable, personal development. An overemphasis on competition and winning will alienate many pupils from sport, especially girls. It might also encourage cheating and an unrealistic importance being placed on being the best. However, sport and games played with an emphasis on the importance of being part of a team or of honouring the traditions of the game might encourage a joyful exuberance at just taking part in a physically active experience. Many children find it difficult to lose, especially when the loss is on display in the public domain. Carefully managed physical education can teach that winners need losers, but losers also need winners, and the game needs both. In fact, both winners and losers have a crucial part to play in allowing a competitive activity to take place. Physical education classes are the ideal place to learn these lessons. Lessons about winning graciously and losing with dignity are too often forgotten in competitive environments. Part of being a complete sporting person is being able to lose as well as win, as the following anecdote shows.

> Laurie absolutely loves soccer. He desperately wants to play for England and win the World Cup. But playing for his primary school team is something of a mixed blessing. All the boys and girls in the team love to play, but they usually end up on the losing side. So we tell them about having fun, and playing for the sake of the game, and being as good as they can be, never mind anybody else. And underneath it all

they enjoy playing but are pretty realistic about their chances of winning, or sometimes even scoring a goal.

It was near the end of the game and they were 4–0 down, but they were pressing hard. The opposition hadn't scored in the second half, and we had told them at half time that they had a chance to win the second half. Anyway, the ball was crossed to Laurie who was unmarked on the edge of the penalty area. I almost wished it hadn't been crossed to him because then, Laurie wouldn't have been expected to score. However, he was in perfect position. He leaned away from the ball, and standing on his left leg, brought his right leg through parallel to the ground and crashed a volley into the corner of the net. 4–1 for the game, but 0–1 for the second half.

Maybe he was lucky to score, maybe they still lost the game, and maybe it won't happen again. Laurie won't play for England and he won't win the World Cup, but at that moment he felt as if he was Michael Owen, Ronaldo and Pele all rolled into one. Laurie had experienced that peculiar joy and exhilaration that sports can bring, at any level of performance. For that experience alone, it was worth all the practices, the disappointments and the defeats. It is also something that, however insignificant it is in the bigger order of things, will be remembered for a long time to come.

One of the major reasons that people take part in sport is the social interaction that occurs in practice, during a game and following it. Most sport and physical education takes place in a social setting, either for the participants, the spectators or both. With the exception of a few activities such as long distance running and swimming, solo climbing, and perhaps walking, all sports and activities are indulged in with others. The role of the 'other' varies but typically could be opponent, partner or team mate. This constant closeness demands certain types of behaviour that will allow the association to continue; in short, antisocial behaviour is unacceptable and would not be tolerated for long. Does this in itself teach participants to act socially? It may of course be that people are naturally social and do not need any refinement of behaviour to operate effectively in a social sporting situation.

Similarly, spectators are in close proximity when viewing sports. The feeling of being part of something greater, and of greater importance, when in a large crowd watching a football match, or the awareness of national identity when a national team performs well in a major tournament are emotions that cannot exist in isolation. They require the existence of others to assume their complete meaning. The most social of sports, rugby, has a tradition of spectators socializing before and after the game that almost supersedes the importance of attending the game itself. Team affiliation does not impede this socializing, so that both sets of supporters can enjoy the event. Spectators at American football games have 'tailgate parties' before games. Here they eat and drink and exchange views on the forthcoming game with other supporters and with supporters of the other team. By its very nature, physical education involves pairs, groups and teams working together. This social interaction is often more informal than in other school subjects, and research has shown that this aspect is attractive to pupils; they approach lessons expecting to socialize.

Sport and its educational counterpart, physical education, thus provide comfortable ways for people to learn, practise and continue social behaviour.

When dealing with the relationship between sport and morality, Arnold (1997) refers to three main theoretical viewpoints: first, the relatively unsupported view that sport builds character; second, that sport is an irrelevance to the serious issues of life and has no effect on character; and third, that sport, particularly professional sport, has a detrimental effect on character development. It should be noted that Arnold is talking here about sport where the importance of winning is predominant and this somewhat slants the discussion. As Rudd and Stoll (1998) point out, it is difficult for high-school, college and professional athletes (in the USA) to be mindful of the finer points of sportsmanship when for years they have been told that winning is of paramount importance. Merely being told to act morally and in a sportsmanlike manner has an abstract quality that nullifies its effectiveness. Moral training, which involves simply being told to do something, needs to be linked to moral education which involves the paticipants in making sportsmanship decisions and carrying out sportsmanlike actions.

If sport is to be used as an educational tool in promoting moral aspects of character, then the notion that sport has fairness as an inherent aspect becomes important. There is an essential difference between sport in schools and sport played outside an educational context. Sport in schools should always have an educational component; it must be used to teach something and to develop the education of the pupils who take part in it. Sport outside educational institutions can fulfil many roles but education is not necessarily one of them: amateur sport is essentially recreation and professional sport is a way of making a living. In other words, professional sport is about winning, amateur sport is about enjoyment and school sport is about learning. This is obviously a simplistic way of identifying the various functions of different levels of sport, but perhaps it offers some clarification of those functions.

Physical education, which uses sport as an educational avenue, has the opportunity to develop the moral, ethical and fairness aspects of sport in a context more likely to achieve such outcomes than sport alone.

Citizenship

Citizenship has a long history as an aim of education. From the days of the Greek city-states to the present day, citizenship has been on the educational agenda. It is now almost as if education has come full circle. Apart from providing the military with fit young men, the main rationale for education in Greek times was to educate the populace for citizenship. Nowadays, citizenship is a serious concern of the government and a number of educational commentators. Following worries about 'levels of apathy, ignorance and cynicism about political and public life and also involvement in neighbourhood and community affairs' (Qualifications and Curriculum Authority, 1998: 4), the Crick report (Qualifications and Curriculum Authority, 1998) was commissioned to report on citizenship and the teaching of democracy in our schools.

A working definition of citizenship would help in our conceptualization of citizenship in education. The Crick report identifies three strands that constitute part of what it is to be a citizen: first, there is a social and moral responsibility; second, there is an element of community involvement; and third, political literacy is seen as desirable in future citizens. Allen (1997) suggests that the rights of citizens cannot be exercised without responsibility. This introduces a type of accountability into being a citizen. If you want the rights that go along with the title, i.e. freedom of speech, access to justice and so on, then you must be willing to defend, exercise and promote those rights. A give and take situation arises where individuals are granted rights by the state in return for compliance with social values and acceptance of responsibility for defence of those norms. In cases of extreme non-compliance with values or non-acceptance of norms the rights can be withdrawn. The existence of such sanctions illustrates society's need for conforming citizens in order for it to be able to operate effectively, and as education is partially about the continuation of society and its values, then the citizenship that is required should be taught and inculcated in schools. This should not be viewed as a negative hegemonic process; rather, it should be recognized as the way that western civilizations operate and maintain themselves.

The historical background and evolutionary story of the National Curriculum gives us some idea of why the idea of citizenship is so important today. During the mid-1980s education in general, and physical education in particular, suffered a great deal at the hands of politicians who used it as an arena in a battle for votes (Kirk, 1992). The combination of an ailing Conservative government and a real concern for the state of education resulted in a campaign to deal with supposedly dangerous, liberal young physical education teachers who were putting our country's sporting future at risk. The wave of popular feeling that was created was to some extent fabricated in order to facilitate the introduction of the National Curriculum as one remedy for the perceived low standards. It was shortly after this period that the curriculum was claimed to promote 'spiritual, moral [and] cultural . . . development' (Department of Education and Science, 1992). So, not only was the government taking on the responsibility for educating the nation intellectually and physically, but it was also stating that it was the business of central government to control spiritual, moral and cultural aspects of children's development. This extension of government control now encompasses citizenship and education for democracy (Qualifications and Curriculum Authority, 1998).

Spirituality

The spiritual element of education was to be taken care of by religious education and the daily act of collective worship. Religious education has been taught in state maintained schools since the Education Act of 1944. This requirement was continued by the 1988 Education Reform Act and, although it is not a core or foundation National Curriculum subject, religious education is seen as part of the whole curriculum. Parents may request that their children do not receive religious education and teachers may request that they do not teach it. Where it is taught, which is in the vast majority of cases, the syllabus must be non-denominational. Although the teaching is intended to be non-denominational, it is an arena where the Anglican church and its associated Christian values can be promoted and assume a privileged position in the spiritual curriculum.

What does spirituality have to do with physical education and sport in schools? For many children the feelings of spirituality that are associated with certain sporting scenarios are far out of reach. How many school children are ever able to stand on top of a high mountain, reach a peak of athletic achievement or watch the sun rise while sailing across an ocean? Unfortunately, the word spirituality has religious connotations that inhibit our thinking. Perhaps rather we should suggest that physical education has the ability to help individuals strive for a euphoric experience, for emotions of goodness and well-being and for oneness with one's physical self. To understand how the body works, to make it work effectively, to treat it with respect and to benefit from the physicality of the body are certainly the results we should expect of school physical education. But 'spirituality' in physical education covers more than just concerns about the body. It also encompasses the notion of feeling good about being physical and feeling good about performing as best one can and physically giving one's all. Physical education does not have a religious component but it may enhance some of the emotions that the religious experience claims to provide.

Many people who compete in endurance events such as triathlons and marathons are overcome with feelings of satisfaction and achievement on completion of these self-appointed challenges, but the ability to put these feelings into words is often lost as elation takes over.

Physical education can also provide a sense of occasion (Blake, 1996), especially when pupils are taking part in large-scale events such as festivals of sport or district competitions. For the few that are privileged to take part in national championhips, there is certainly an emotional feeling of being special, of being a part of something bigger.

The popular tendency to extend the argument further and suggest that sport is like a religion in some countries is a rather limited view, and one that takes no account of the sustainability of the religious experience. Much religious doctrine is concerned with existence after life on earth has finished, whereas sport is concerned with the here and now. Although one might remember spiritual sporting experiences years after they have happened, there can be no pretence that sport benefits our afterlife. Physical education and sport enhance our existence now and are to be valued for that alone.

The feelings of utter despair and total exhilaration that sporting failures and successes can bring allow us to experience these emotions in the fairly safe environment of the sporting arena. With a few extreme exceptions, such as climbers and yachtsmen, nobody dies because of sporting success or failure. However, in real life these feelings can often only be triggered by major life events such as birth and death. The detached experiencing of these emotions is one of the attractions of sports and games; we can go through the emotions with none of the real consequences, but we can touch on the spirituality of life and existence.

We had spent ten days gradually ascending to 15,000 feet, the height of our 'base camp', before we go over the pass. Everybody had coped very well, although we'd had the odd blister, or tummy bug but nothing serious. We were all pretty fit after ten days walking and acclimatising to the heat, and then to the cold and the altitude. On our way up, we have seen some of those who haven't made it. Some on mules and some walking back down, there's no other way to go. We all have secret hopes of being OK, and secret fears of not being OK. The night before I had really bad headaches so I had to take some Diamox. I was so pleased to wake up at 4 a.m. with a clear head. It was −10 degrees centigrade and very dark, but clear and still star speckled. Today we are going over the pass, 18,000 feet.

We begin after a breakfast of noodle soup and chocolate. At first we have head torches to light our zig-zag way up the path. I find it very slow going and quite breathless, but not impossible. About half way up, after a couple of hours, the sun begins to light the Annapurnas, first pink then yellow and finally white. Up and up we go, past a couple of false summits, through some mini ice fields, and at last we are at the top. At 18,000 feet we are surrounded by the high tops of mountains on all sides. The sun is warm but the air is cold and clear. The breathing returns to normal and I take some photos, and I begin to think of the circumstances and the chain of events that have brought me to this place, and tears begin to run down my cheeks.

Hundreds, possibly thousands, of people trek the Annapurna circuit every year, and most of them cross Thorung La. I'm sure that most of them have some sort of emotional experience. And although, even at the summit, we are surrounded by higher peaks, we feel as if we have all climbed our own individual mountain.

(Author's personal diary, 1999)

Britain is not alone in this call for spirituality to be recognized as a function of education. There are similar movements in the USA towards a return to a more value-based system (Palmer, 1998). It seems that the technocratic education of the 1970s and 1980s has not adequately met the demands of society. There is now a perception that there is something more to education than just learning facts about things. Hence there has been emphasis on the ideas on citizenship, moral education, character development and so on. The sense of dissatisfaction can be traced back to the mid-1980s and the 'Great Debate' about education concerning whether or not it was adequately fulfilling its social function. We are living today with the manifestation of the changes that were instigated at that time.

Morality

Moral aspects of the curriculum are closely linked to citizenship, although at the time of the Education Reform Act education for citizenship had not been fully conceptualized. The social and moral responsibility suggested as a first strand of citizenship by the Crick report fits very well with what the National Curriculum is required to deliver now, and will be required to deliver in the future. Society wants young people who know right from wrong, who behave in a moral way, and who support a moral code that enables large numbers of people to live effectively together. Sport, as a microcosm of society, can help with inculcating these moral aspects. It has often been stated that playing team games, or any other games, teaches people to play by the rules and to adopt the conventions of fair play. But one only has to watch professional sport on television to know that this is not always the case. However, in educational circumstances children can easily be taught the fair way, that is, the right way, to play games. They can be taught that playing by the rules allows the game to take place for everyone's benefit. In the larger context, this translates into everyone, or at least the vast majority of people, obeying the law of the land to allow society to function. In general terms, this is what happens. Some people cheat and are devious in their dealings with others, but the majority of people 'play the game' and are fair and law abiding. This cannot be attributed solely to the lessons of physical education. But physical education plays a part in the process as an element of a complete education.

Acculturation

Crick does not mention the cultural aspect of citizenship, but the National Curriculum states that it is important that young people know about the society and the culture in which they live. This covers vast stretches of knowledge, custom, history and tradition, from the definition of an acceptable amount of personal space to the knowledge that England won the World Cup in 1966; from the custom of shaking hands to knowing that the Beatles were from Liverpool. The sharing of common knowledge, customs and traditions is part of what defines a society and a culture. It has already been established that sport, sporting tradition and legend is an important part of culture. The notion of a well-rounded individual dictates that, in addition to literacy and numeracy and all the other intellectual abilities, an individual must be adequately knowledgeable about a number of topics. Thus not only is mental intelligence developed, but so also is musical intelligence, physical intelligence, cultural intelligence and all the other intelligences. Thus the concept of citizenship can be seen to be close to that of the 'Renaissance man'. A balanced human being who appreciates the arts and sciences, can enjoy conversation about a number of topics, but has no knowledge of the sporting arena would be limited in social interaction because of the importance that society places on sporting culture. Therefore, we can say that a person who has not developed their physical intelligence is not fully educated.

Sport as a part of popular culture has been examined earlier, and in many other texts: the significance of sport is not at issue. To be a citizen requires an understanding and acceptance of the culture in which one exists and sport is an integral part of that culture. Many of the sports taught at schools in physical education are part of the tradition of this country. Those that are not can also provide enrichment by showing that other cultures value sport and have something to offer the sporting cultural arena. This increases the diversity of ethnic experience. Exposure to school physical education and school sport is not a prerequisite for sporting acculturation, but it certainly facilitates and expedites that process.

Community involvement

The Crick report's second strand in the definition of citizenship is community involvement. It is recommended that pupils learn about and become involved in the concerns of their communities. This should include service to the community.

Schools do not exist in a vacuum. Their context inevitably represents their physical and socio-economic surroundings. Schools are part of the larger community because they are physically in the community. However, although many secondary schools also carry the title of Community College, how many can truly be said to be fully integrated with the community? The provision of evening classes and encouraging adults into daytime classrooms is not sufficient to make that school part of a community.

The contact that most people have with a school is either as a pupil or as a parent. The school is no more of a community centre than the church, the pub or the village hall. All can claim to act as centres for different sectors of the community but there is no single one that can be regarded as the centre of the whole community. What schools can offer as an advantage over other locations is an extensive array of facilities. Classrooms, assembly halls, computer suites and sports facilities are all on site at schools. Some schools do allow extensive use of their facilities outside traditional school hours, and some of the school facilities that receive the most use are the sports facilities. But all that this means of course is that the school as a facility is part of the community; it does not mean that the pupils are involved in the local community.

There is a potential source of confusion in the fact that pupils live in the community that the school serves and thus are already part of that community. Why do they then need to be told how to be part of that community? One of the ways in which pupils can begin to appreciate the value of community and neighbourhood is through their school's involvement in the community.

What is difficult for most pupils, and indeed for most people, is to view the school as an integrated part of the greater community and not as a separate place where children go to receive an education. Schools that establish real links with their communities are obviously better placed to achieve integration than those that exist in isolation. Schools can be daunting places; this is especially true of secondary schools because of their size. Many parents and adults see no reason to ever go to schools. They have experienced school from a pupil's perspective but have very little awareness of the way a school is run, what the working life of a teacher is like or of the expanded place and purpose of a school in a community.

We can all be teachers and we can all be learners. While not demeaning the training, education and work of school teachers, it is important to recognize that many people in the community have much to offer children. Schools often welcome adults other than teachers into classrooms to share their experiences and special skills. This is not a 'mums' army' of do-gooders, but an educated, concerned group of individuals who are a welcome aid to the ability of schools to provide an inclusive and well-rounded education. Helping with sports teams, specialist skills in the arts and extending foreign language are just some of the ways in which expertise from outside school can be used.

Schools should also go out into the community to seek out new experiences for their pupils. These visits already happen but they need to be made more explicit; schools should be openly saying 'we have this expertise and these "teachers" in our neighbourhood'. When we look for places that children can learn, we begin to realize that school is only one of those places and that 'teachers' are everywhere.

Schools tend to be better at acting upon the realization that learners are not just those who physically attend school than at seeking out alternative learning environments for their pupils. Many schools have extensive community education programmes to meet many of the educational needs of their communities. However, the connotations of the label 'school' and the 'emotional baggage', both good and bad, that most people carry as a result of their childhood experience of school, limit and define which of them are attracted back as non-traditional learners. It would perhaps be too easy and trite to suggest that the only people who are attracted back to community education programmes are the middle classes, for whom the value of education has been demonstrated and for whom school was a rewarding experience. But a large segment of the population have little intention of ever returning when they leave the school premises for the last time as a pupil. This highlights two problems. First, the education they have received as school pupils has had very little relevance to their lives as adults. Second, the community education programme does not offer what they want or need. I believe the question needs to be asked, why is there a notion that we all have to be lifelong learners? Can we not accept that if contentment, satisfaction, health and happiness can be achieved and maintained, there should not necessarily be a requirement to continue to learn.

One of the ways in which schools serve the greater community of which they are part is to instil in pupils the sense that they form part of a global community of learners. Sport has a place in this. Sportspeople around the world have a common 'language', a common foundation of interest and a sharing of the sports experience that link them into a global sports community. Part of the role of physical education is to teach children this common 'language', to instil interest and to provide opportunities for this sports experience to take place. The learning of skills, knowledges, values and attitudes is merely a vehicle that allows pupils to take their place in the global community of sport. Just as a school working effectively in a community can promote a sense of belonging to a community, so physical education and school sport can help to develop a sense of belonging, in the global sporting context. This can provide an affiliation missing from many young people's lives; they can be provided with a 'sense of place' and a feeling of belonging (Stiehl's third domain of responsibility, environmental). They can begin to establish a sporting identity, and this locates them in the sporting and recreational context which constitutes part of our global community.

Many schools have community outreach programmes which allow pupils to volunteer and help in the local area. Many schools also have twinning arrangements and links with schools in other countries, in Europe and worldwide. These links often involve sporting encounters and, though probably not the most important, sport is a valuable part of such relationships, providing a vehicle for contact and interaction.

Political literacy

The third strand of Crick's citizenship definition is political literacy. The report suggests that pupils need to become effective in the life of the nation. Knowing about democracy is not enough; pupils ought to learn to practise democracy. To understand how our society functions children need to know about the political and legal system at all levels of operation, from parish council to European and international agencies. As Allen (1997) suggests, children need to know how the political becomes personal; how their lives are affected by what councils and governments do, and also sometimes by events on a global as opposed to a local scale. This naturally leads to knowing about contemporary issues that affect the way we live and think.

Is it possible for sport and physical education to help in this process, or should sport and physical education not even attempt to become involved in political education? The way sport itself operates is not renowned for being democratic. Rather, it is seen as autocratic both in the way it is run and also in the way teams, sportsmen and women, and coaches operate. The coach in particular is generally viewed as an autocratic figure often more so than the teacher. Some sports, such as American football and gymnastics, are dominated by the coach, while others, such as orienteering and cricket are less so. In physical education lessons most teaching is didactic and takes the form of command. So sport and physical education do not seem to form a natural arena for witnessing democracy at work. However, there are events in and around sports that demonstrate a democratizing process in action. For example, the Bosman ruling that allows footballers to change clubs with far more freedom at the end of their contract exemplifies a movement towards democracy in football. There are also examples where sports events demonstrate that sport is far from being democratic, such as the boycotts of the 1980 and 1984 Olympics and the implementation of apartheid in South Africa.

Although physical education may not have a clearly defined role in contributing to political literacy, it can provide examples of democracy, and the lack of it. For children who enjoy sports and games, examples relevant to these interests, such as those above, could stimulate awareness that the exercise of democracy as a part of political literacy is not far removed from their own lives and interests.

It is suggested that citizenship could be taught with subjects such as history and geography. Physical education has a major contribution to make in this cross-curricular area. When this is linked to the new emphasis on personal, social and health education, there is an overwhelming case for the importance of physical education to be recognized and awarded the relevant status in the school curriculum.

The answer to this chapter's title is now unequivocally clear. Physical education for the new millennium is a subject of expanded boundaries and possibilities. Those possibilities include the promotion of responsibility, the encouragement of personal development and a contribution to the education of a community of global citizens.

7 The 'Once and Future' Subject

Some Current Issues in Physical Education

The underlying subtext of this book has been that 'traditional' physical education as we know it is uncontextual, does not meet the needs of the pupils and is missing its potential to be an agent for change and good in a developing education system that is now asking much more of its subjects than just teaching pupils facts and skills. It has already been made clear that education for the new millennium requires not only subject content expertise in pupils, but also the production of fully developed and well rounded 'citizens' of society, including its extended global community. With moral education, cultural awareness, spiritual awakening, character development and citizenship coming into prominence, are we looking at the return of 'Renaissance man'? If this is the case then we need to realign our subject to meet these new demands. We need to take account of the subject's latent potential, already discussed, relax the constraints of 'performance pedagogy' and take our subject into a new era of holistic education. Physical education and sport in schools are uniquely placed to take a leading role in this 'education for the next century'.

Although I am sure that the physical education and sports community would welcome increased prominence for physical education and sport, certain conditions need to be met before that future role can be completely developed. Many of these 'conditions' involve finding solutions to the problems that face the subject in schools today. So before the potential of our subject can be released, society and the sporting community need to recognize and attempt to solve some of these existing problems.

Politics and Educational Initiatives

Unfortunately, the solutions to many of the issues which physical education confronts are in the hands of politicians, who do not have a good track record in dealing with physical education. Before the implementation of the National Curriculum, there was a feeling within the profession that the subject had been marginalized and undervalued. Although the National Curriculum ensured the survival of the subject, many in the profession cannot forget the way that the forces of the political right used physical education as a pawn in marshalling public support for the Education Reform Act of 1988. And many of the problems facing the subject today are a result of a series of political interventions. An example is the decreasing time available for physical education, particularly in primary schools: there is considerable pressure on schools to produce pupils with better literacy and numeracy skills, and intiatives such as the 'literacy hour', although good for literacy, cause problems in that time has to be taken away from other subjects. Physical education falls into the category of subjects, along with art, music and the other humanities, that have been marginalized.

As the 'challenges' facing the subject are explored it will become apparent which are the result of government intervention – and therefore need government action to help resolve them – and which can be resolved by the actions of concerned professionals in the education arena.

Self, Personal Growth and the Promotion of Self-Esteem

There are many conditions that must be evident and existing before we can say that a child is ready or prepared for learning. We are told that pre-school education 'prepares' a child for learning at primary school. We are told that constructive play with parents and siblings 'prepares' a child for the rough and tumble of playground and school life. These pre-conditions are desirable in that they can optimize the opportunities that then present themselves in formal schooling and can provide some of the tools for learning. However, there is one pre-condition that is not often mentioned, but which needs to be considered as a condition of prime importance, especially in the light of the arguments presented so far. Simply put, it is that children must feel good about themselves before they can learn effectively. Taken to an extreme for the sake of illustration, if children are worried about their home life, or bullying, or have poor self-esteem, or think that their lack of ability might be exposed in lessons then these feelings take priority and learning becomes difficult at best, and irrelevant at worst. On the other hand, children who feel good about themselves and have good self-esteem are in a far better position to take advantage of learning situations. As adults we know that a lack of distractions helps us to concentrate. Why should it be any different for school children? We also know that it is children's perceptions of the physical education experience in schools that makes a major contribution to determining whether they will go on to be active adults (Fox, 1988b). A good feeling about oneself is therefore crucial to healthy and active lifestyles, one of the aims claimed for physical education. The case is easily made: good experiences of school physical education lead to good self-esteem; this leads to a positive perception of physical activity, which in turn can lead to a healthy, active lifestyle, thereby diminishing the risk of obesity and coronary heart disease and resulting in a healthier population.

One of the links in this chain is self-esteem which is one of the components of 'self' that sport and physical education claim to be able to develop and improve. Other components of 'self' that require some examination are self-concept and self-confidence. All three are linked in a complicated matrix of interdependences that creates a complete 'self'.

Self-concept

Self-concept is the view, or visual image, that one has of oneself. This can most easily be defined by a series of descriptive statements, such as, 'I am male', 'I am white', 'I am a sportsman', 'I have a good physique' and so on. With these statements a picture is constructed of that person's view of themselves. If the picture constructed matches the real picture, then we can say that a person has a good self-concept. Unfortunately, this is not always the case. The most obvious example of a poor self-concept is the anorexic who has such poor body image that it threatens their very survival. The anorexic's picture of her (very occasionally his) body is a one of fatness and overweight, even though she may in fact be painfully thin. When this is linked to an overwhelming desire to be slim or thin, the anorexic ignores what her eyes tell her and relies on a faulty self-concept, which as a result can be very damaging. There is a strong argument that social conditioning makes a big contribution to this desire to be thin, for we are surrounded by images of slim and attractive women in magazines and on billboards. Increasingly, we are faced with similar images of men, although these tend to concentrate on a muscular appearance. The 'six-pack' stomach is now an image of desirability, fitness and attractiveness for many young men.

This suggests that the self-concept is not something that comes entirely from within. We see what are considered attractive physiques all around us and we are constantly told that health and fitness are important for a prolonged existence.

In terms of development in young children, this has important ramifications for our subject. Children learn first to define themselves in the light of what they see themselves to be (Lee, 1993). They measure their abilities according to whether or not they can do something. It is only later that children take into account what other people think and say and do. They then begin to measure what they look like against other children and also they start to evaluate their abilities against those of other children. Children who develop a good image of themselves and have more physical ability than most generally develop a good self-concept. But this measurement against others hinders those who are less able. Later still, children begin to see what society says people should look like, what physical attributes and skills are important, and what value is placed on traits of intelligence, physical ability and looks. Children who have poor self-concept and a lack of strength and support to resist such a bombardment of cultural expectations then suffer increasingly, the worst manifestations of which develop into pyschological and physical disorders such as anorexia.

School sport and physical education can assist in helping the child to develop a good self-concept and in resisting the damaging, pervasive images of society's demands. Not all children can be good at sports, but all children can be encouraged to like and appreciate some element of sports. It might be that some children like to play football, whereas others might like to do another activity to keep fit. Some might like to play badminton and others might like to referee matches, or coach, or be knowledgeable spectators. There is something good in physical education and sports for nearly everyone. This is illustrated by the growing interest in Paralympics worldwide and, in the USA, in the Special Olympics. These arenas provide the opportunities for disabled people to take part, to be acknowledged, and for a few, to excel at sports. The trend towards inclusive physical education in Britain shows just how important it is that all children should have that opportunity. Nearly every child should be able to derive something from their school physical education experiences to benefit their self-concept.

For those who value their performance in games and sports, the measure of success needs to be realistic and attainable. By definition, only a few gifted athletes in any group of school children will experience success, and thus a boost to their self-concept, if success is measured only as being superior to other children. Unfortunately, the stage of development where assessment of one's ability is made against the ability of others tends to coincide with the time that children start to learn together and play together in schools. It therefore becomes very difficult for teachers to encourage task orientation in children so that they evalaute their performance against the task set, or against their own prior performance on the task. Although it might be difficult for teachers to achieve this, the attempt should be made because the rewards are worth the effort. Imagine a class of children where they all had a good self-concept, were not disappointed by traditional ideas of failure but valued their worth because they had done their best, achieved their potential and had all found something in sport that was important to them. That aim is not an unreasonable one for the whole of school physical education.

Self-confidence

Another aspect of self is self-confidence. As self-concept grows and increases in accuracy and stability it is likely that self-confidence will develop. If self-concept is a reliable awareness of one's appearance and abilities, then self-confidence is a belief in one's appearance and abilities. Self-confidence is an inbuilt conviction that one will do well and be successful. The following anecdote shows how self-confidence can be achieved.

When Harry first tried to read, he hesitated for a long time before making an effort. I immediately understood why. In addition to having a specific learning difficulty (dyslexia) Harry had a violent stutter. Not only could Harry not understand the words, he couldn't actually say them. From that day on we didn't ask Harry to read out loud unless he wanted to have a go. Harry really didn't have a lot going for him, and we struggled to find something he enjoyed and could experience some success at. He didn't like stamp collecting, he was artistically challenged, he was OK at sport but he wasn't going to set the world alight, but he did like cricket. The thing he liked most was bowling. He was average, but for him that was quite an achievement! He practised and played when he could, he began to enjoy life at school a bit more. He also began to try to read out loud sometimes. Gradually he improved, both at cricket and with his reading. His stutter started to go as he became more comfortable, more at home, and more confident in his ability. Eventually, Harry got into the school team in his last year with us.

Harry's crowning glory came on his last day of school. There was a school against staff cricket match. All the parents were watching, maybe 200 people in all. The staff needed six runs to win, I was batting, Harry was bowling. He ran up, pitched one short, I hooked it to the square-leg boundary, but Harry had placed a fielder there and I was caught out. The school won the game and Harry was a hero. Later that day Harry made a short speech in front of the 200 people without a single hesitation. The applause was deafening.

Sport did not eliminate Harry' stutter, but it certainly improved the quality of his school experience. It gave him a certain amount of confidence that he was able to carry over into other areas of his life. Harry went on to become a successful stockbroker. I think he still plays cricket.

Measures of success

Lee (1993) suggests that setting the appropriate goals ensures prior success and thus leads to an improvement in self-confidence. So development is progressive and must be built sequentially to ensure solid foundations. This idea is obviously somewhat context-specific: self-confidence when taking part in physical education lessons might not be transferred completely to situations of greater stress, increased competition and more importance such as county or national championships. This is referred to as situational self-confidence. Thus, the differing status of the sporting setting will have some effect on self-confidence. A child or adult who is physically gifted and has good physical self-confidence in one area is likely to be able to transfer that confidence to other physical activities. So a good football player is likely to feel able to perform fairly well in most team sports. It does not always follow that the participant will be able to perform well. It does not follow either that a person who has good self-confidence in sports will be confident in their ability in music or literature or art. Self-confidence is domain-specific for most people. Some will feel confident about their ability in sports, while others will feel confident about their ability in mathematics or the arts, and so on. However, there are some supremely confident individuals, a few of them extremely talented, who are self-confident across the spectrum of domains and in a variety of settings. These people offer a benchmark of quality that might also have been appreciated in Renaissance times: as an individual who has developed their talents in all areas of endeavour to the best of their ability and to the best of their education. Perhaps such models of intellectual, physical, social and moral growth and development ought to be held up as aspirational icons for the educational system.

Self-esteem

The final component of self is self-esteem. Self-esteem is defined as an awareness of good in oneself when measured against a self-imposed standard. In practice however this self-imposed standard is constructed according to a variety of influences, just as the self-concept is developed in a contextual way. So self-esteem, although it is an individual trait, has a large element of social construction and can be affected by the actions of teachers and others to benefit that aspect of the child's development.

The most attractive explanation of the way self-esteem is constructed follows the hierarchical model. In this model, ability in a small component of a sport, such as the serve in badminton, contributes to the next level of the model, which is the way a person feels about their ability at the sport of badminton. This in turn contributes to the next level in the hierarchy, which might be general sports ability or physical self-esteem. Other components at this level could be intellectual, social and emotional self-esteem (Fox, 1988b).

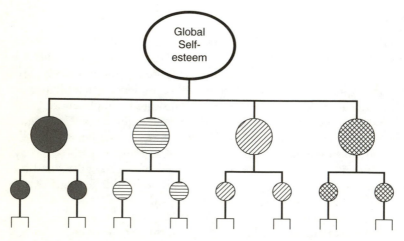

Figure 7.1 Hierarchical model of self-esteem structure

This model supersedes earlier proposals such as a unidimensional model where all component parts contribute equally to one overall measure of self-esteem and a multidimensional model in which it was recognized that varying components had different importance and each component was weighted so that it contributed to overall self-esteem according to its importance to the subject. Unfortunately, not all teachers have recognized that these models are now somewhat antiquated.

Global Self-esteem

Figure 7.2 Unidimensional model of self-esteem structure

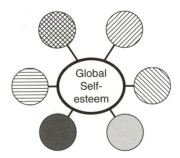

Figure 7.3 Multidimensional model of self-esteem structure

It is vitally important that teachers of physical education and coaches in sporting situations involving young people have some knowledge of the hierarchical model of self-esteem construction. Armed with this knowledge they will be able to encourage youngsters to value what they are good at and either discount what they are less good at or help them to improve their skills in areas of lesser ability. At the same time teachers and coaches must be prepared to adopt alternative measures of success for the majority of pupils who do not experience success using traditional measures. This redefinition of success does not mean that physical prowess is any less valued. It does mean that other opportunities for personal success should be provided, or at least recognized (Fox and Biddle, 1989). Just achieving a skill is, for some, as much a personal success as winning a contest is for others. Developing fitness in a health-related fitness programme and learning to referee a football game might constitute success for some pupils and such non-traditonal measures needs to be recognized, encouraged and provided for.

In addition to an expansion of opportunities for success there can also be a refocussing of pupils' success orientations. Comparative assessment against one another or against a norm is not very helpful for the majority of children, as it merely ensures that the they fail or that they are aware of falling short of what is expected. It would be far better if a system of personal goals were adopted and pupils were encouraged to set themselves reasonable targets, with the teacher's help, against which they would measure their progress at some future date. This would give youngsters a sense that their goals were attainable and, as Fox and Biddle (1989) suggest, an increased sense of personal control. Hopefully, with this increased personal control will come a feeling that the curriculum is of personal relevance.

The notion of building the 'self' and promoting personal growth through physical education and sports has a very simple basis. Young children are physically active: they run, jump, climb trees and climbing frames, play tag and so on because they like it. Similarly, adults who lead active lifestyles do so because they like it and obtain a sense of satisfaction from taking part in physical activity. By using alternative measures of success, by redefining what is meant by success, and by developing the growth of a positive self-esteem within the activity, teachers can help children and young people to find that sports and physical activity give them a sense of fulfilment and satisfaction that will encourage them to carry on with an active lifestyle.

The practicalities of how this can be done are not really the province of this book, but it is worth noting what Fox and Biddle (1989) have to say on how the subject should be approached in general. They highlight four of the areas that have already been mentioned as crucial to developing effective physical education programmes that will fulfil their objectives. (Currently, a high drop-out rate and low participation levels indicate that many programmes fall short of that aim.) First, we need to provide more chances of success for more of our pupils, and more opportunities for them to perceive that they have had success. This obviously covers a wide range of possibilities, from merely participating to competing and winning – and of course sometimes losing! Unfortunately, continued political emphasis (Department of National Heritage, 1995) has created a central spine in physical education curricula consisting of purely competitive games. (Incidentally, this emphasis privileges the male notion of what constitutes games and physical education at the expense of the female concept of the subject.) Physical education therefore needs to reinvent itself to take account of a number of personal requirements that its participants bring to the gymnasium. This reinvention would include components that cater more for the needs of individuals than to the mass dissemination of physical knowledge that society, by way of a politically motivated working party, has deemed should be seen as the school subject. As mentioned earlier, it needs to be recognized that the subject is not just about doing physical activity and games, but offers a range of opportunities and roles that pupils can be encouraged to fulfil if current physical education leaves them unsatisfied and demotivated.

Fox and Biddle's second suggestion is that we create the right kind of success for our youngsters. They again criticize the fact that traditional physical education is so performance based that it is hard to measure success in any other way. The indicators of performance are in the public domain and as such are easily assessed. They are also usually used to measure performance against that of other pupils or against some sort of norm-referenced criteria. In either case participants are being assessed against a measure outside themselves. Pupils need to be encouraged to concentrate on personal goals, as opposed to achievement that depends upon external comparisons, in order to allow all to have a reasonable chance of success. They will then see that the achievement of a different kind of success can rest with them and be within their power, while not being dependent on anyone or anything else.

The third point made by Fox and Biddle is that we must create the desire to take part. This is closely linked to the relevance of the curriculum. However, the subject benefits from generally positive attitudes towards it in the primary years and in the early secondary years. From adolescence onwards participation declines and attitudes become more negative and less supportive towards the subject. The reason for this has never been satisfactorily answered. It is generally assumed that since there are more options on offer and increasing demands on pupils' limited time, that pupils have increased spending power and an awareness of the wider world, these factors combine to decrease participation and interest in school physical education. It is not very popular to suggest to teachers that their 'clients' no longer want what is on offer. Put bluntly, physical education in the later secondary years is largely seen by its participants as irrelevant, boring and unnecessary. Making adolescents play football, hockey or cricket (all competitive games) for the eleventh year running is not a good way to persuade them of sport's relevance to their lives and existence. At this age, unless pupils enjoy and gain some satisfaction from what they do, they will not want to do it for very long. Our current curriculum fails to create the desire to participate at this stage except in a very few.

Last, Fox and Biddle explain that pupils must have the knowledge that enables them to make rational choices and decisions about physical activity. This adds to the argument that physical education is about more than just performing; it is about doing, knowing, feeling and valuing, and so on.

Unfortunately, much of the foregoing bears little relation to many physical education programmes in schools today. This is not a criticism of schools and physical education professionals, but rather of the political construction of the National Curriculum in physical education. Teachers are able to teach games and skills very well; they are good technical educators. This is what is required of teachers in schools by the demands of the National Curriculum. Unfortunately, they are not so good at promoting values and attitudes because they are not taught how to do it, nor are they held accountable for promoting these aspects as they are for producing physical improvements in pupils. What the government says must be provided is only partially successful in meeting the needs of pupils. Perhaps the way forward is to make these individual needs more of a priority, while the needs of society will continue to be met as a result of a generation that values physical activity, takes pride in a cultural background of sporting achievement and endeavour and has the skills and knowledges needed to make rational choices about maintaining physically active lifestyles.

Access, Provision of Opportunity and Equality

What we do as sportspeople is conditioned by a whole raft of circumstances and experiences. Socialization into sport is an area of study in its own right and provides us with a wealth of information which suggests that our choice of sports is determined by a combination of parental interests and encouragement, peer and 'significant other' interests and opportunity. While society can do very little, if anything, about the first two, society can have a large effect on the opportunities available to, and provided for, young people.

Much of the research to date (Hargreaves, 1994; Clarke and Humberstone, 1997) has dealt with the issue of gender when addressing the equal provision of opportunities. Although this issue is still alive, much has been achieved by the tremendous struggle by concerned writers and activists which has helped women's sport reach the point where it is now. Fortunately, girls and young women now have female role models to enhance and give a focus to their sporting aspirations (Robbins, 1999: 13). It is also apparent that female sports performance has progressed so far and so fast that the level of achievement in some areas is fast approaching that of the men – this is particularly true in endurance events such as long distance running and swimming, and triathlon. Progress is not solely due to the appearance of role models. An awareness of the lack of equality of sports opportunities and the structural inequities in physical education programmes has led to many of these problems being addressed. Women now have the chance to play rugby, to use an often quoted example. Many more school clubs have been provided to take account of young women's wishes to take part in different types of extra-curricular sports, and the active, fit, young woman has become something of an icon in the world of fashion and lifestyle magazines.

However, there is another side to the story that often goes unmentioned. Because of the great strides that have been made it might seem churlish to make further complaints, but only by highlighting problems can they start to be addressed. Let us take the above scenarios to illustrate how seemingly encouraging examples hide underlying difficulties. More women play rugby; there are more women's rugby clubs and more girls are playing and enjoying tag rugby in schools. This is obviously good for girls and women as well as good for rugby and indicates that schools are making efforts to accommodate the changing interests of their students. However, there are still very few women's rugby clubs and in some parts of the country there are none. This naturally prevents some women continuing with their sporting interests. Tag rugby is very popular in the primary schools where the staff have been trained and are confident to teach it, although there are still many schools where this is not the case. However, when pupils progress to secondary education the opportunity for the girls to continue with rugby is much more rare. So girls are encouraged to play rugby at an early age and develop an interest but are sometimes unable to pursue it because the avenues for progression do not exist at school or in the community.

In a similar way the provision of school clubs catering for girls' sport is dependent on a variety of factors such as the availability of staff and facilities, staff interest and expertise, and the numbers of girls that take up the opportunity even if it is provided. These constraints constitute a powerful force for the maintenance of the status quo in sports provision, despite the best efforts of concerned and conscientious individuals. In fact, structural and practical constraints of school life demonstrate the subtle, and often unintentional, ways in which a patriarchal hegemony is pursued and promoted. Even with the best intentions, which includes equality of sports club provision and the same opportunities for girls as for boys, the promotion of girls into non-traditional sports is extremely problematic, perhaps even to the extent of insolubility. Sporting culture is male dominated and has underlying it a mindset that is resistant to change. The improvements listed above are only a start and need a great deal of impetus from concerned parties to achieve a situation in which both halves of the population enjoy the same opportunities. But there is now at least acknowledgement that sporting education should be available equally to all, regardless of sex.

All of the above argument assumes the absence of external factors such as climate and geography that can influence opportunity provision. However, we live in a real world where training and participation in many outdoor sports are hindered by poor weather conditions. Furthermore, some regions of the country are better provided for in general in terms of sports facilities. And some sports are more popular in some parts of the country than in others. If sport tries to be all things to all men, it sets itself an almost impossible task, and therefore invites failure. A great diversity of factors limit and determine the type of provision and opportunity available and we must be realistic in what we can expect to achieve in terms of identical provision and opportunity across the board. Perhaps the best that can be achieved is that all segments of society – gender groups, ethnic groups, religious groups or age groups – have the same equality of provision and opportunity as other segments of society, and it is the case that equity awareness in sports and physical education has improved enormously in the last forty years. Women have opened the doors, allowing many other groups to become equal partners in the sporting world.

The politics of access

The issue is complicated even further by conflicting messages in government documentation concerning the school sports arena. When *Sport: Raising the game* (Department of National Heritage, 1995) was first published, the sporting community believed that they were, at last, being taken seriously in political terms and that school sport was being given priority in the education world. Many sportspeople welcomed the solid backing of the prime minister. A closer reading and a more analytical interpretation gives a very different message, however. Gilroy and Clarke (1997) provide a devastating criticism of John Major's proposals. They claim that what was being proposed was simply a relaunch of a traditional view of sport and physical education. That is, that sport and physical education are based around team games. Much was made of the social and moral development that is possible through sport (the very point of this book) but there was a vast underlying assumption that this development was only possible using the 'authorized' view of what constituted sport. The fact that other activities had as much, if not more, to offer in this regard was completely ignored. This privileging of a certain type of physical education creates further problems in that it is far from gender equitable. It is well known that competition in sports is enjoyed by boys far more than it is by girls. This deeper analysis sheds a very different light on a superficially beneficial initiative.

Additional criticism aimed at John Major claimed that it was the Conservatives who had 'run down' school sport through lack of funding in the first place and therefore it was hypocritical for them now to blame teachers of physical education in particular, and schools in general, for a perceived lack of sport in schools. The government's marshalling of the views of the populace to support what appeared to be a very reasonable proposal bears remarkable similarities to the tactics of the Thatcher government of the mid-1980s (Kirk, 1992), when physical education and young teachers were identified as the reason for a decline in British teams' performances in international competition. When politicians want them to, sport and physical education can have a very high profile indeed.

A further example of a political initiative that used sport for its own advantage is the establishment of some schools as specialist 'sports colleges'. Once again, such a proposal seems on the surface only to offer benefit to all concerned. These establishments are meant to be focal points for excellence in sports, not only for the children at the school, but also for the local and regional community. They seek to improve teaching and learning in physical education for children of all abilities, to develop links between schools, sports bodies and communities and to promote participation at all levels. Many of these schools employ specialist coaches to work with groups in their target sports. Some provide strong links with primary schools in their catchment areas. Others seek to provide a structure through which young people involved in elite sports can progress. All these ambitions are admirable and it would be wrong not to recognize that an enormous amount of good should come of such a programme of support and funding: in addition to improved facilities, there will increased opportunities for young people, a higher status for the subject within the school and a higher status for the physical education staff. All concerned will see that their subject and interest is being held in high esteem and is being viewed as something important, to be promoted and valued by the school and the surrounding community. Thus it would seem that everybody wins: at whatever level they participate, youngsters will be encouraged into sport through an increased emphasis on school physical education.

However, we need to consider the messages that specialist sports college status sends to the various segments of the school's constituency. We also need to consider the sustainability of the initiative. In global terms we are again seeing the privileging of one subject within the school curriculum. Although this is good for physical education, why should it disadvantage other subjects? There are other types of specialist colleges – technology colleges and language colleges being two examples – but all schools cannot be specialist in all subjects. This singling out of a subject within a school is therefore problematic in terms of equity between subjects. There has long been an unwritten hierarchy of subjects, with English, mathematics and the sciences holding high status positions, but this hierarchy has evolved through a process involving history and tradition: thus it has come about naturally and has achieved a balanced ecology of the different subjects that is maintained and sustainable but at the same time changeable when subject to natural forces. A government imposed alteration to this balance offers a false perspective. Physical education will be seen as important because of the political initiative, not because of its inherent worth and value to the school. As a result, the increased status of the subject is probably not viable in the long term.

We also need to ask what this increased profile suggests to youngsters who are not good performers in physical education, or who do not enjoy the sports that have been targeted by the school, or those who excel at another subject not deemed to have special status. Are their interests, aspirations and talents of less value and importance than those of their sporting colleagues? Even if schools make every effort not to make these implications obvious and public, these messages are implicit in the very existence of the scheme. Does a school that is a specialist sports college place as much value on musical ability and achievement? Can a school that targets hockey place as much value on ability in rugby? And does a school that promotes elite performance do so to the disadvantage of average and below average sports performers? To date these questions have not been asked, let alone answered. Everyone and every subject is considered equal – it's just that some are more equal than others!

A third issue is that of sustainability. Although the Youth Sport Trust, the body appointed to liaise with specialist sports colleges, has a commitment to continuing professional development (Whelan, 1998) and on-going evaluation, there appears to be no indication of the time span intended for the initiative, beyond the intitial three-year development plan. The danger is that, in common with many political programmes, it will be subject to the whims and political expediency of the government of the day. There is a possibility that, schools having made a huge commitment in terms of time, staff, expectations, facilities and equipment, the political climate might change and the initiative may no longer be seen as viable. If support is there now, however, schools might seem foolish to ignore the opportunity to benefit from such a development. But a note of caution needs to be sounded, so that whatever a school puts in place as a result of special status can be sustained without the continued support of the government, the Youth Sport Trust or the donations of local private sponsors.

These questions for discussion do not imply that the initiative is totally flawed, however. As indicated earlier, for children, staff and schools interested in sports through physical education, the provision of specialist status is a wonderful opportunity. All need to be aware nevertheless that these good things have implications that need to be dealt with effectively in order not to disadvantage as many as are privileged.

Activity Levels, Health-related Exercise and Curriculum Time

Activity levels

Physical education and sports have many positive aspects, among the most powerful of which is the fact that they deal with the areas of play, games and recreation. Young children indulge in play and games for the fun of them. People become knowledgeable about their sport and value their own participation as an end in its own right. There needs to be no other justification for taking part other than one's enjoyment, but an additional reason is found in the idea of activity for lifelong fitness recommended by theorists and researchers, and known as 'body maintenance'.

Fitness is now a multi-million pound industry. The number of health clubs, fitness centres and lifestyle clinics has increased enormously in recent times. The clothing industry now caters for this market with work-out gear and leisure clothing and some very expensive training shoes. Also available are various types of weights, running machines, rowing machines, and cycle machines that are meant to make keeping fit more accessible, easier and more fun. The message is proclaimed by magazines for women, men and teenagers and by lifestyle magazines: be active; be fit; be healthy; look good and live longer. This media message has probably done more to increase participation in health producing exercise for adults than school physical education. What emerges is the fact that the physical education system has the expertise, the facilities and the mandate to influence the activity decisions of young people but that it does not have the 'street cred' that would make young people take notice. This notion is supported by the wealth of research showing that young people, particularly adolescents, have low levels of activity.

Armstrong and McManus (1994) pose the following questions: are British children and adolescents fit; are they active; are activity and fitness related in this population; and do early activity patterns relate to activity in adulthood? They used the results of their previous studies to attempt to provide answers to these pertinent questions. It has been assumed that children's fitness levels are deteriorating, but this is only partially borne out by the findings. Cardiopulmonary fitness and blood pressure were found to be satisfactory, but too many children were overweight and poor blood lipid levels (indicating unsatisfactory cholesterol levels) were common. It was found that boys were more active than girls and that boys' levels of activity did not change much with age. Girls, however, decreased their physical activity as they got older. Overall, there were very low levels of habitual physical activity and many children do not do enough excerise to promote, improve or maintain health. One would expect that the more moderate to vigorous physical activity (MVPA) that a child did, the fitter he or she would be. (MVPA is defined as activity that requires at least as much effort as brisk walking.) Armstrong and McManus (1994) found no such relationship. Difficulties in assessing genetic influences on fitness and in establishing a relationship between fitness and activity prevented any generalizations in this area from being made. The researchers cite Kuh and Cooper (1992) and the *Allied Dunbar National Fitness Survey* (Sports Council and Health Education Authority, 1992) as providing evidence that above average ability and activity in childhood led to the likelihood of more active lifestyles in adulthood. This represents a considerable challenge for physical educators in schools. If average ability appears not to be enough on its own to encourage activity into adulthood, then perhaps enjoyment could at least persuade more individuals to persevere and develop better abilities. In summarizing their findings, Armstrong and McManus emphasize the importance of promoting and encouraging more activity among children and adolescents.

Sleap and Warburton (1994) observed a sample of children aged 5 to 10 to determine their activity levels. The observations were carried out during school break times, physical education lessons and school lunch times; there were also observations during free time outside school. The researchers were mainly concerned with periods of MVPA and periods of sustained activity. They found that children engaged in MVPA for about 30 per cent of the time and that there was no difference between boys and girls. Although this might seem to contradict the findings of Armstrong and McManus (1994) it should be remembered that Sleap and Warburton were looking at primary-school age children. Differences in activity patterns do not tend to make themselves evident until later, perhaps as influences outside their immediate environment begin to have an effect on behaviour.

Sallis and Patrick (1994) list the activity guidelines suggested by the International Consensus on Physical Activity Guidelines for Adolescents (covering 11 to 21 year olds). Thirty-four invited experts summarized the health benefits of activity and made two recommendations. First, adolescents should be physically active daily, or nearly every day. What form the activity takes is not prescribed but it could conceivably be school physical education, family recreation, games, play or even work, such as digging the garden.

The second guideline suggested that adolescents should engage in at least three periods of MVPA that last twenty minutes or more each week. Examples of this would include, but not be limited to, brisk walking, playing football, swimming laps and cycling. It is apparent from this list of suggestions that this is where the difficulties lie. While the first guideline could easily be incorporated into normal life without too much problem, the second requires a definite commitment to activity for it to be implemented, but as we know commitment to activity declines as adolescents get older.

The Health Education Authority (HEA, 1998) made similar recommendations for activity in young people (5 to 18 years old). First, all young people should take part in physical activity of moderate intensity for one hour a day, qualified by the suggestion that inactive children could begin with half an hour a day. Moderate intensity is defined as activity that leaves the participant slightly out of breath, such as brisk walking. As can be seen, the HEA recommendation is very similar to the first 'consensus' guideline, although there are minor differences in time prescription and definition.

Second, the HEA suggests that at least twice a week, some activities are done to promote strength, flexibility and bone health. The 'consensus' suggests that this type of activity should be done three times a week. Activities of this type include climbing, weight-bearing activities such as gymnastics, or sports such as basketball.

Both sets of recommendations are similar in that they operate on two levels. First, there is the 'lifestyle' promotion of daily activity, and second, there is the type of activity programme that will produce a training effect such as muscular strength and bone health. The recommendations are also similar in that they mention social, psychological and moral benefits that may be derived from regular activity. The 'consensus' statement says that significant beneficial psychological effects can be obtained after training three times a week for ten to fifteen weeks. The HEA report maintains that physical activity can enhance psychological well-being, self-esteem, and moral and social development. The development of self-esteem is particularly evident in disadvantaged groups and those with initial low self-esteem, but there is a caution added that overemphasis on competitive performance can limit these benefits. Although both of these significant reports are primarily concerned with issues of physical health in young people, it is encouraging to note that there is a strong recognition of the greater good that participation in physical activity can bring.

Health-related exercise

The case has already been made that we are witnessing a boom in the sport and recreation world. We are also increasingly aware of the importance of an active lifestyle in sustaining health and promoting social develpment. Apart from a curriculum that includes physical education, in what ways are our schools making use of this increased impetus? The most obvious answer, and perhaps the one that has generated the most debate, is in the development of health-related exercise (HRE) initiatives.

Although health-related exercise does not appear as a separate area of activity in the National Curriculum, it is written into the programmes of study at all four Key Stages. Schools and teachers are left to decide for themselves what is the best way to impart the required information. It is suggested that in some instances HRE is best delivered in lessons focussing on aspects of the programme. At other times it might be more appropriate for the information to be offered as an integral part of normal physical education lessons. There are arguments to support both methods. A series of lessons dedicated to HRE lends weight and importance to the concepts being taught and discourages the distraction of other lesson content. On the other hand, applying principles of HRE to sporting and physical education situations might aid the pupils in seeing the relevance of the material in practical ways.

A broader perspective is adopted by Almond and Harris (1997) when they provide some practical guidelines for teachers. In addition to the behavioural components of HRE, such as adopting physical activity as a lifestyle and taking opportunities to be active, they promote the affective and cognitive components. In the cognitive domain they include safety in exercise and knowledge of the role of exercise. The affective area is suggested in developing love of activity, recognition of its value, and enhanced enjoyment and confidence in participation. It can now be recognized that even supposedly technical and individually based initiatives, have a real benefit in addition to the psychomotor and the body maintenance/fitness benefits.

Cale (1996) echoes these ideas when she reports that teachers' ideas, and the ideas of others, are changing with regard to HRE. No longer is there a common view that it is all about circuit training and running.

Instead it is recognized that children must be encouraged to value activity for itself not just for the benefits that it can bring. She also begins to dispel the myth that HRE is anti-sport, anti-competition and anti-performance. Harris (1998) takes up this theme and lists some ways in which HRE contributes to physical education in schools. She lists the cognitive aspects of knowing about exercise and its effects on the body, about how to exercise safely and so on. Exposure to different activities such as walking, aerobics and personal workouts, that might be more appropriate to active lifestyles than traditional physical education activities can offer significant benefits. She also concludes that HRE can enhance self-esteem and self-confidence in activity environments. Harris goes on to describe a physically educated person. In doing so she virtually mirrors the description by the National Association for Sport and Physical Education (NASPE, 1992) (see p. 16). According to Harris, a physically educated person is one who has learned the necessary physical skills, participates regularly, understands the implications of being active and values the contribution of activity to a healthy lifestyle. Among her recommendations to help schools promote physical activity are suggestions for community involvement, provision of social environments that are encouraging and enjoyable, and the establishment of a whole-school approach.

The adoption of a whole-school policy is also mentioned by Cale (1997). She provides a conceptual framework in which to locate the rationale for school HRE policy. This includes the school ethos, the curriculum (both formal and informal), links to the community, the environment, and also care and support structures. Many of these concepts are the same as those discussed in relation to physical education and school sport's contribution to developing responsible individuals and rational citizens. This connection of healthy individuals and healthy societies is perhaps the best argument there is for physical activity, whether it is in schools, families, communities or globally. It seems that whatever cause is being advanced, sport can be involved to some degree or another, invariably in a beneficial way. We seem to be getting closer to an holistic approach to education and it seems that physical education is being viewed as a perfect vehicle for much that is proposed.

Curriculum time

In addition to the worry over activity levels of children, there is concern in the physical education teaching profession over decreased curriculum time available for the subject. This decrease in allocated time has been well documented over the last few years, although actual figures vary according to which report is consulted. This is because of differences in sample size, regional variations and individual interpretations by different schools before the introduction of curriculum guidelines. Nevertheless, time for physical education has diminished.

A report by the Physical Education Association as long ago as 1987 documents a reduction in curriculum time in secondary schools from a weekly average of 170 minutes in 1974 to an average of 116 minutes in 1986. In twelve years the time had fallen from nearly three hours a week to just under two hours a week; a reduction of one third. A closer inspection of the figures shows that the reduction was by far the greatest in year 11, which is the GCSE year, and in the sixth form where pupils are studying for A levels and other advanced public examinations. So schools were falling short of the recommended minimum of two hours a week (Department of National Heritage, 1995), nine years before it was recommended. The reduction is continuing: Harris (1994) reports that the time allocation has shrunk to 109 minutes a week. In addition, Fairclough and Stratton (1997) found that in years 10 and 11 (Key Stage 4, ages 15 and 16) physical education had only 80 minutes a week. Harris (1993) reports an even worse case, with 75 minutes a week for the same age group.

The pattern we see in secondary schools is quite clear; less time being allocated to physical education across the board. And just at the time when adolescents are making lifetime choices, many involving recreation and leisure, their physical education time in schools is being particularly reduced. The messages implied, such as 'Do as we say not as we do' or 'Activity is important, but we haven't got time for it', are not encouraging.

Schools in the primary sector vary in respect of time allocated for physical education. In 1995–1996 it ranged from one and a half to two hours a week (Clay, 1997). This brevity was compounded by the fact that where there was less time for physical education, the teaching standards were also lower. So the children who had the least physical education also had the worst teaching. At a stage when we hope to teach basic skills and instil fundamental attitudes, our youngest school children are clearly being deprived of what they deserve and have a right to.

The United Kingdom fares badly in a comparison with other European countries (Armstrong and McManus, 1994). At primary level, schools in the United Kingdom have the least time allocated to physical education of any European country. Switzerland, Spain, Portugal, Norway and Austria all have about three and a quarter hours a week, whereas the United Kingdom has about one and three quarter hours a week. At secondary level, only Ireland has less time, with one and a quarter hours a week. At the other end of the table, Switzerland, Portugal, Spain and France have about three and a quarter hours of physical education a week in secondary schools.

What emerges is a pattern of contradiction. All the documentary evidence from curriculum theorists, policy writers, government initiatives and educational trends indicates that school sport and physical education have a huge role to play in the development of rational individuals as well as in the local and global communities. However, the affective areas of the subject that are at the heart of such development receive very little real attention.

The subject itself is also being cut back and marginalized in such a way that even the performance and psychomotor aspects of the curriculum are extremely difficult to achieve. It is clear that, given these problems, the potential of physical education and school sport is being compromised and a subject that can offer so much is delivering little, as a result of circumstances beyond its control.

However, because the issues raised here are of great public concern, and because of the trends involving personal, social and health education and citizenship, there is a glimmer of hope that physical education and sport may yet fulfil their potential as agents for change and contributors to a better and richer lifestyle for their participants.

8 Conclusion

The boundaries of physical education as a school subject have been clearly drawn, the precise position of the role of sports in schools has been defined and what teachers and pupils do in lessons and on the sports field has been examined. This has brought us to a clear understanding of the state, status and place of physical education and sports in schools today. The pedagogy of educational practice dictates how the subject is taught, the values that are promoted and the attitudes and knowledges that are instilled in young people throughout the process of education. The current situation is the result of an historical development that has been well documented. Change is constant, and so change continues. Change must be viewed as an opportunity to build a more philanthropic pedagogy.

This book has tried to explore the idea of an increased role for physical education and sport and thus inspire the reader with the future possibilities for the subject area. The subject boundaries need to be pushed back and attitudes need to change towards a more inclusive education, where affective and social outcomes are embraced with the same enthusiasm with which we now embrace the teaching and development of physical skills. This will enable the true potential and complexity of the subject to be addressed and realized.

We need to evolve our traditional pedagogies into ones that are liberating and empowering. This will remove us from the safe and comfortable but ultimately restricting pedagogy of the didactic, into one characterized by an holistic approach to educating the individual and recognition of responsibilities on a global scale. This will enrich the discipline and produce an end product that is worthwhile in many differing contexts. The combination of philanthropic pedagogy and expanded content will allow the subject to become a valuable instrument for the development of the whole individual.

An harmonious partnership in the subject between the learning of physical skills and the acquisition of personal and social skills broadens its appeal, which is especially important in an era of increasing time pressure on curriculum subjects. The ability to integrate learning outcomes should be cross-curricular but physical education and sport offer a unique opportunity to address affective dimensions. These now include the concept of citizenship, and this book has shown how a 'citizenship' strand could easily be adopted in curriculum physical education. This corresponds neatly with the ideal of building a society where the notion and value of 'community' is necessary for the education of socially responsible youth. If this can be achieved it might become a valuable tool for preventing basically good youngsters from making bad decisions.

However, it is not just education in schools that needs to be examined. If we are prepared to embrace the future of physical education, we need to change the way we train the teachers of the future. There must be a broadening of what constitutes teacher education to include the ideas discussed here. This will require a cultural shift that enables 'performance pedagogy' to include 'humanistic pedagogy' thus becoming a complete, cohesive eclectic pedagogy. This will at last bridge the gap between the technocratic, skill development school of thought and the personal, social and moral school, thereby enhancing the individual's whole self while at the same time promoting the best of physical performance. We know that we can train very good teachers of skills so there is no reason why we cannot adapt the training to include the affective areas. The new suggestions for the inclusion of personal, social and health education and the promotion of citizenship mean that this will become a necessity. It would certainly be to the benefit of the subject, and the profession, if physical education could be pro-active instead of reactive in responding to changes; if it could for once be 'ahead of the game'.

Finally, the work of other disciplines can help the profession to progress in this manner. The notion that learning is an active occupation and is located in social and cultural contexts has been elaborated. When this is linked to developmental models of curriculum (e.g. the National Curriculum and Hellison's responsibility model) it becomes clear that physical education in schools is founded on a constructivist approach to learning. Physical education is used to teach more than just the physical and a multiplicity of purposes fits well with constructivism. Kirk and Macdonald's (1998) adoption and application of situated learning theory to physical activity settings provides a fresh approach that facilitates further exploration of alternative pedagogies in physical education and sport. They demonstrate particular concern with the context, relevance, content and method of teaching physical education.

There are two concepts in situated learning theory that have an attraction for the future development of the subject. First is the idea that activities take place in different communities of participants and that the location and the community condition what can be expected and achieved. So we might have a school location with teachers and school children, or a community sports centre location with coaches and players, and each of these will have meanings and associations attached that mediate the experience for the participants. The second concept is one of legitimate participation. This suggests that the participation must have some sort of meaning and purpose for the individual in order to be legitimate. It is suggested that participants move through a series of activity communities before becoming full participants with expertise and experience in any particular activity. This is clearly demonstrated in schools and most sports settings where the power of the relationship rests firmly with the teacher or coach, in that he or she is the holder of the knowledge that is needed for learners to become full participants in the sports community.

It can now be seen that school physical education falls short of helping pupils to become full participants in the sporting community. Kirk and Macdonald (1998) point out that health-related fitness, Hellison's social responsibility model and sport education are all attempts to address these perceived shortcomings. Unfortunately, there is a powerful ideology that maintains school physical education as an educational version of 'game playing'. But there are reasons to hope that changes are afoot.

Personal, social and health education will be promoted as an important part of education for the new millennium. This text has demonstrated that school physical education can play a large part in satisfying this curriculum requirement, thus contributing both to the whole school curriculum and to the personal development of individuals. The notion of citizenship is something with which all schools will have to deal in the near future. School sport and the larger, global community of sport can engender positive relationships within sports activities and between participants that has been shown to carry over into life outside sport.

While physical education and sport cannot claim to be the sole vehicles for a new holistic, humanist education, they can begin to exploit their potential in this area and take the lead in pushing education forward into an age where the process and the outcomes merge into a complete and meaningful educational experience. The practicalities of such an enterprise will need to be addressed in teacher education programmes and in teaching in schools. In this book I have tried to provide a theoretical basis and background of research from which can be developed the next generation of physical education in schools and sport activity for young people in general. In this way, physical education can be promoted as a subject that really does go 'beyond the boundaries'.

References

Aicinena, S. (1991) The teacher and student attitudes toward physical education. *Physical Educator*, Winter, 28–32.

Allen, G. (1997) *Education at risk*. London: Cassell.

Almond, L. and Harris, J. (1997) The ABC of HRE: Translating a rationale into practical guidelines. *British Journal of Physical Education*, 28(3), 14–17.

Armstrong, N. and Biddle, S. (1992) Health-related physical activity in the National Curriculum. In N. Armstrong (ed.), *New directions in physical education. Volume 2*. (pp. 71–110). Leeds: Human Kinetics Books.

Armstrong, N. and McManus, A. (1994) Children's fitness and physical activity: A challenge for physical education. *British Journal of Physical Education*, 25(1), 20–26.

Arnold, P. J. (1997) *Sport, ethics and education*. London: Cassell.

Arrighi, M. A. and Young, J. C. (1987) Teacher perceptions about effective and successful teaching. *Journal of Teaching in Physical Education*, 6(2), 122–135.

Bain, L. (1975) The hidden curriculum in physical education. *Quest*, 24, 92–101.

Bain, L. (1985) The hidden curriculum re-examined. *Quest*, 37, 145–153.

Bandura, A. (1977) *Social learning theory*. Englewood Cliffs, NJ: Prentice-Hall, Inc.

Beglin, A. (1968) Some sources of conflict in the role of the physical education specialist. *The Leaflet*, 69(10), 89–90.

Berstein, B. (1975) *Class, codes and control (Volume 3). Towards a theory of educational transmission*. London: Routledge and Kegan Paul.

Blake, B. (1996) Spiritual, moral, social and cultural development in physical education. *Bulletin of Physical Education*, 32(1), 6–16.

Bloom, B. (1980) The new direction in educational research: Alterable variables. *Phi Delta Kappan*, 61, 382–385.

Borg, W. R. and Gall, M. D. (1989) *Educational research: An introduction*. New York: Longman.

Brohm, J.-M. (1978) *Sport: A prison of measured time*. London: Ink Links.

Cale, L. (1996) Health-related exercise in schools: P.E. has much to be proud of! *British Journal of Physical Education*, 27(4), 8–13.

Cale, L. (1997) Physical activity promotion in schools: Beyond the curriculum. *Pedagogy in Practice*, 3(1), 56–68.

Carlisle, C., Phillips, D. A., Cochran, J., Hermanson, J., Lindsay, B., Powell, K., Rohwer, J., Rushing, G., Shetty, A. and Souza, W. (1984) An analysis of the relationship between student attitude and student achievement. Unpublished paper, University of Northern Colorado, Greeley.

Carlson, T. B. and Hastie, P. A. (1997) The student social system within sport education. *Journal of Teaching in Physical Education*, 16(2), 176–195.

Carroll, B. (1994) *Assessment in physical education: A teacher's guide to the issues*. London: Falmer Press.

Cheffers, J. (1973) The validation of an instrument designed to expand the Flanders system of interaction analysis to describe non-verbal interaction, different varieties of teacher behavior and pupil response. Unpublished doctoral dissertation, Temple University, Philadelphia, PA.

Clark, G. H. (1971) A process of obtaining information and attitudes of children regarding elementary school. Unpublished doctoral dissertation, Columbia University, New York.

Clarke, G. and Humberstone, B. (1997) *Researching women and sport*. London: Macmillan Press.

Clay, G. (1997) OFSTED reports. *The Bulletin of Physical Education*, 33(1), 52–58.

Coakley, J. J. (1994) *Sport in society: Issues and controversies*. St Louis, MO: Mosby-Year Book Inc.

Coe, J. (1984) Children's perceptions of physical education in the middle school. *Physical Education Review*, 7(2), 120–125.

Crum, B. J. (1985) The use of learner reports for exploring teacher effectiveness in physical education. In M. Pieron and G. Graham (eds), *The 1984 Olympic scientific congress proceedings. Volume 6. Sport pedagogy*. (pp. 97–102). Champaigne, IL: Human Kinetics.

Darst, P., Zakrajsek, D. and Mancini, V. (1989) *Analysing physical education and sport instruction*. Champaigne, IL: Human Kinetics.

Delamont, S. (1983) *Interaction in the classroom*. London: Methuen.

Department for Education. (1995) *Physical education in the National Curriculum* (Statutory Orders). London: Her Majesty's Stationery Office.

Department of Education and Science. (1977) *Curriculum 11–16*. Working papers by HM Inspectorate: A contribution to current debate. (p. 80). London: Her Majesty's Stationery Office.

Department of Education and Science. (1992) *Physical education in the National Curriculum*. (Statutory Orders). London: Her Majesty's Stationery Office.

Department of National Heritage. (1995) *Sport: Raising the game*. London: Department of National Heritage.

Dibbo, J. and Gerry, S. (1995) Physical education meeting the needs of the whole child. *British Journal of Physical Education*, 26(1), 26–27.

Dickinson, B. and Sparkes, A. (1988) Pupil definitions of physical education. *British Journal of Physical Education, Research Supplement*, 2, (n.p.).

Doyle, W. (1979) Classroom tasks and students' abilities. In P. L. Peterson and H. J. Walberg (eds), *Research on teaching: Concepts, findings, and implications*. Berkeley, CA: McCutchen Publishing Co.

Dunkin, M. J. and Biddle, B. J. (1974) *The study of teaching*. New York: Holt Rinehart and Winston.

Dyson, B. P. (1995) Students' voices in two alternative elementary physical education programs. *Journal of Teaching in Physical Education*, 14(4), 394–407.

Earl, L. M. and Stennett, R. G. (1987) Student attitudes toward physical and health education in secondary schools in Ontario. *Journal of the Canadian Association for Health, Physical Eduction and Recreation*, 53(4), 4–11.

Edgington, C. W. (1968) Development of an attitude scale to measure attitudes of high school freshmen boys toward physical activity. *Research Quarterly*, 39(3), 505–512.

Ennis, C. D. (1985) Purpose concepts in an existing physical education curriculum. *Research Quarterly for Exercise and Sport*, 56(4), 323–333.

Ennis, C. D. (1990) Analyzing curriculum as participant perspectives. *Journal of Teaching in Physical Education*, 9(2), 79–94.

Erickson, F. (1982) Taught cognitive learning in its immediate environments: A neglected topic in the anthropology of education. *Anthropology and Education Quarterly*, 13(2), 149–180.

Fairclough, S. and Stratton, G. (1997) Physical education curriculum and extra-curriculum time: A survey of secondary schools in the north-west of England. *British Journal of Physical Education*, 28(3), 21–24.

Fernandez-Balboa, J.-M. (1993) Sociocultural characteristics of the hidden curriculum in physical education. *Quest*, 45(2), 230–254.

Fink, J. and Siedentop, D. (1989) The development of routines, rules and expectations at the start of the school year. *Journal of Teaching in Physical Education*, 8(3), 198–212.

Fisher, C. W., Filby, N. N., Marliave, R., Cahen, L. S., Dishaw, M. M., Moore, J. E. and Berliner, D. C. (1978) *Teaching behaviors, academic learning time and student achievement: Final report of phase III-B, beginning teacher evaluation study.* Washington, DC: National Institute of Education, Department of Health, Education and Welfare.

Flanders, N. A. (1960) Interaction analysis in the classroom: A manual for observers. Minneapolis, MN: College of Education.

Flanders, N. A. (1970) *Analyzing teaching behavior.* Reading, MA: Addison Wesley Publishing Co. Inc.

Flintoff, A. (1991) Equal opportunities and practical assessment in examination PE: Part 2. *British Journal of Physical Education*, 22(1), 35–37.

Fox, K. (1988a) The child's perspective in physical education. Part 1: The psychological dimension in physical education. *British Journal of Physical Education*, 19(1), 34–38.

Fox, K. (1988b) The child's perspective in physical education. Part 5: The self-esteem complex. *British Journal of Physical Education*, 19(6), 247–252.

Fox, K. and Biddle, S. (1989) The child's perspective in physical education. Part 6: Psychological and professional issues. *British Journal of Physical Education*, 20(1), 35–38.

Gelfand, D. M. and Hartman, D. P. (1978) Some detrimental effects of competitive sports on children's behavior. In R.A. Magill, M. J. Ash, and F. L. Smoll (eds), *Children in sport: A contemporary anthology.* (pp. 196–206). Champaigne, IL: Human Kinetics.

Gibbons, S. L. and Bressan, E. S. (1991) The affective domain in physical education: A conceptual clarification and curricular commitment. *Quest*, 43(1), 78–97.

Gibson, J. H. (1993) *Performance versus results: A critique of values in contemporary sport.* Albany: State University of New York Press.

Gilroy, S. and Clarke, G. (1997) Raising the game: Deconstructing the sporting text – from Major to Blair. *Pedagogy in Practice*, 3(2), 19–37.

Greendorfer, S. L. (1987) Psycho-social correlates of organized physical activity. *Journal of Physical Education, Recreation and Dance*, 58(7), 59–64.

Griffin, P. (1984) Girls' participation patterns in a middle school team sports unit. *Journal of Teaching in Physical Education*, 4(1), 30–38.

Griffin, P. (1985) Boys' participation styles in a middle school physical education team sports unit. *Journal of Teaching Physical Education*, 4(2), 100–110.

Grineski, S. (1989) Children, games, and prosocial behaviour: Insight and connections. *Journal of Physical Education, Recreation and Dance*, 60(8), 20–25.

Gruber, J. J. (1986) Physical activity and self-esteem development in children: A meta-analysis. In G. A. Stull and H. M. Eckhert (eds), *Effects of physical activity on children*. (pp. 30–48). Champaigne, IL: Human Kinetics.

Guttman, A. (1978) *From ritual to record: The nature of modern sports*. New York: Columbia University Press.

Haan, N. (1991) Moral development and action from a social constructivist perspective. In W. M. Kurtines and J. L. Gurwitz (eds), *Handbook on moral behavior and development: Volume 1. Theory*. Hillsdale, NJ: Erlbaum.

Hammersley, M. and Woods, P. (eds) (1984) *Life in school: The sociology of pupil culture*. Milton Keynes: Open University Press.

Hargreaves, A. and Woods, P. (eds) (1984) *Classrooms and staffrooms: The sociology of teachers and teaching*. Milton Keynes: Open University Press.

Hargreaves, D. (1975) *Interpersonal relations and education*. London: Routledge and Kegan Paul.

Hargreaves, J. (1986) *Sport, power and culture: A social and historical analysis of popular sports in Britain*. Cambridge: Polity Press.

Hargreaves, J. (1994) *Sporting females: Critical issues in the history and sociology of women's sport*. London: Routledge.

Harris, D. (1973) *Involvement in sport: A somatopsychic rationale for physical activity*. Philadelphia, PA: Lea and Febiger.

Harris, J. (1993) Physical education in the National Curriculum: Results of a pilot study in secondary schools. *British Journal of Physical Education*, 24(4), 36–40.

Harris, J. (1994) Physical education in the National Curriculum: Is there enough time to be effective? *British Journal of Physical Education*, 25(4), 34–38.

Harris, J. (1998) Health-related exercise: Rationale and recommendations. *British Journal of Physical Education*, 29(3), 11–12.

Hastie, P. A. (1995) An ecology of a secondary outdoor adventure camp. *Journal of Teaching in Physical Education*, 15(1), 79–97.

Health Education Authority. (1998) *Young and active: Policy framework for young people and health-enhancing activity*. London: Health Education Authority.

Hellison, D. R. (1978) *Beyond bats and balls: Alienated (and other) youth in the gym*. Washington: American Alliance for Health, Physical Education, Recreation and Dance.

Hellison, D. R. (1983) It only takes one case to prove a possibility...and beyond. In T. J. Templin and J. K. Olson (eds), *Teaching in physical education*. Champaigne, IL: Human Kinetics.

Hellison, D. R. (1985) *Goals and strategies for teaching physical education*. Champaigne, IL: Human Kinetics.

Hellison, D. R. (1987) The affective domain in physical education: Let's do some housecleaning. *Journal of Physical Education, Recreation and Dance*, 58(6), 41–43.

Hellison, D. R. (1996) Teaching personal and social responsibility in physical education. In S. J. Silverman and C. D. Ennis (eds) *Student learning in physical education: Applying research to enhance instruction*. Champaigne, IL: Human Kinetics.

Hendry, L. B. (1975) The role of the physical education teacher. *Educational Research*, 17(2), 115–121.

Hendry, L. B. and Welsh, J. (1981) Aspects of the hidden curriculum: Teachers' and pupils' perceptions in physical education. *International Review of Sport Sociology*, 16(4), 27–40.

Huizinga, J. (1955) *Homo Ludens: A study of the play element in culture*. Boston, MA: Beacon Hill Press.

Inglis, F. (1977) *The name of the game: Sport and society*. London: Heinemann.

Inglis, F. (1985) *The management of ignorance*. Oxford: Blackwell.

Jewett, A. E. (1978) Aims and objectives in physical education: Subject matter and research methods of sport pedagogy as a behavioral science. In H. Haag (ed.), *Sport pedagogy content and methodology*. Baltimore, MD: University Park Press.

Jones, B. (1988) Attitudes of school pupils to curriculum physical education. *British Journal of Physical Education, Research Supplement*, 3, (n.p.).

Karabel, J. and Halsey, A. H. (eds) (1977) *Power and ideology in education*. New York: Oxford University Press.

Kenyon, G. S. (1968) Six scales for assessing attitude toward physical activity. *Research Quarterly*, 39(3), 566–574.

Kirk, D. (1992) *Defining physical education: The social construction of a school subject in postwar Britain*. London: Falmer Press.

Kirk, D. (1993) Curriculum work in physical education: Beyond the objectives approach? *Journal of Teaching in Physical Education*, 12(3), 244–265.

Kirk, D. (1995) Action research and educational reform in physical education. *Pedagogy in Practice*, 1(1), 4–21.

Kirk, D. and Macdonald, D. (1998) Situated learning in physical education. *Journal of Teaching in Physical Education*, 17(3), 376–387.

Kirk, D. and Tinning, R. (1990) Introduction: Physical education, curriculum and culture. In D. Kirk and R. Tinning (eds) *Physical education, curriculum and culture: Critical issues in the contemporary crisis*. London: Falmer Press.

Kleiber, D. A. and Roberts, G. C. (1981) The effects of sport experience in the development of social character: An exploratory investigation. *Journal of Sport Psychology*, 3, 114–122.

Kuh, D. J. L. and Cooper, C. (1992) Physical activity at 36 years: Patterns and childhood predictors in a longitudinal study. *Journal of Epidemiology and Community Health*, 46, 114–119.

Laker, A. (1995a) Effective teaching behaviours of physical education student teachers. *Bulletin of Physical Education*, 30(3), 54–63.

Laker, A. (1995b) Physical education lessons in England: Content and perceptions. *Proceedings of ICHPER.SD 38th World Congress*, Gainesville, FL, USA. July, 1994.

Laker, A. (1996) Learning to teach through the physical, as well as of the physical. *British Journal of Physical Education*, 27(4), 18–22.

Lambdin, D. D. and Steinhardt, M. A. (1992) Elementary and secondary physical education teachers' perceptions of their goals, expertise, curriculum and students' achievement. *Journal of Teaching in Physical Education*, 11(2), 103–111.

Lawson, H. A. (1986) Occupational socialization and the design of teacher education programs. *Journal of Teaching in Physical Education*, 5(2), 107–116.

Lee, M. (1993) (ed.) *Coaching children in sport*. London: E & FN Spon.

Loadman, A. (1998) Marginalised children in the primary school: Masculine hegemony and physical education. *Journal of Sport Pedagogy*, 4(2), 1–11.

Mangan, J. A. (1981) *Athleticism in the Victorian and Edwardian public school.* Cambridge: Cambridge University Press.

Martens, R. (1975) *Social psychology and physical activity.* New York: Harper and Row.

Martinek, T. (1988) Confirmation of a teacher expectancy model: Student perceptions and casual attributions of teaching behaviors. *Research Quarterly for Exercise and Sport,* 59(2), 118–126.

Martinek, T. (1989) Children's perceptions of teaching behaviors: An attributional model for explaining teacher expectancy effects. *Journal of Teaching in Physical Education,* 8(4), 318–328.

McGuire, J. and Thomas, M. H. (1975) Effects of sex, competence and competition on sharing behaviour in children. *Journal of Personality and Social Psychology,* 32, 490–494.

McMillen, B. (1992) An analysis of factors associated with student responses to instructional tasks in physical education. Unpublished doctoral dissertation. University of Northern Colorado, Greeley.

Mechikoff, R. and Estes, S. (1993) *A history and philosophy of sport and physical education: From the ancient Greeks to the present.* Madison, WI: WCB Brown and Benchmark.

Meek, G. A. and Smith, M. D. (1998) A field study of supervisory intervention of preservice physical educators via data-based feedback: Feeding back feedback. *Journal of Sport Pedagogy,* 4(1), 43–55.

Mercier, R. (1992) Beyond class management: Teaching social skills through physical education. *Journal of Physical Education, Recreation and Dance,* 63(6), 83–87.

Metzler, M. (1989) A review of research on time in sport pedagogy. *Journal of Teaching in Physical Education,* 8(2), 87–103.

Milosevic, L. (1996) Pupils' experience of PE questionnaire results. *British Journal of Physical Education,* 27(1), 16–20.

Morgan, W. J. and Meier, K. V. (eds) (1988) *Philosophic inquiry in sport.* Champaigne, IL: Human Kinetics.

Morris, G. S. D. and Stiehl, J. (1998) *Changing kid's games.* Champaigne, IL: Human Kinetics. (2nd edition).

National Association for Sport and Physical Education. (1992) *Outcomes of quality physical education programs.* Reston, VA: American Alliance for Health, Physical Education, Recreation and Dance.

National Association for Sport and Physical Education. (1995) *Moving into the future: National standards for physical education. A guide to content and assessment.* St Louis, MI: Mosby.

National Curriculum Council (1990) *Curriculum guidance 3. The whole curriculum.* York: National Curriculum Council.

Oslin, J. L., Mitchell, S. A. and Griffin, L. L. (1998) The game performance assessment instrument (GPAI): Development and preliminary validation. *Journal of Teaching in Physical Education,* 17(2), 231–243.

Palmer, P. J. (1998) The grace of good things. *Sun,* September, 24–28 (USA).

Patrick, C. A., Ward, P. and Crouch, D. W. (1998) Effects of holding students accountable for social behaviors during volleyball games in elementary physical education. *Journal of Teaching in Physical Education,* 17(2), 143–156.

Phillips, D. A. and Carlisle, C. (1983) A comparison of physical education teachers categorized as most and least effective. *Journal of Teaching in Physical Education,* 2(3), 55–67.

Phillips, D. A., Carlisle, C., Steffen, J. and Stroot, S (1986) The computerised version of the Physical Education Teacher Asessment Instrument. Unpublished manuscript, University of Northern Colorado, Greeley.

Physical Education Association of Great Britain and Northern Ireland. (1987) *Physical education in schools*. Report of a Commission of Enquiry. London: Physical Education Association of Great Britain and Northern Ireland.

Placek, J. H. (1983) Conceptions of success in teaching: Busy, happy and good? In T. J. Templin and J. Olson (eds), *Teaching in physical education*. (pp. 46–56). Champaigne, IL: Human Kinetics.

Pollard, A. (1988) Physical education, competition and control. In J. Evans (ed.), *Teachers, teaching and control in physical education*. (pp. 109–124). London: Falmer Press.

Portman, P. A. (1995) Who is having fun in physical education classes? Experiences of sixth-grade students in elementary and middle schools. *Journal of Teaching in Physical Education*, 14(4), 445–453.

Pritchard, O. (1988) Attitudes towards physical education in England: An investigation among parents, pupils and teachers. *Physical Educator*, Fall, 154–156.

Qualifications and Curriculum Authority. (1998) *Final report of the Advisory Group on Education for Citizenship and the Teaching of Democracy in Schools*. London: Qualifications and Curriculum Authority.

Rice, P. L. (1988) Attitudes of high school students toward physical education activities, teachers and personal health. *Physical Educator*, 45(2), 94–99.

Robbins, T. (1999) Superwomen athletes get set to make men also-rans. *Sunday Times*. March 14, 13.

Rosenshine, B. V. and Furst, N. (1971) Research on teacher performance criteria. In B. O. Smith (ed.), *Research in Teacher Education*. (pp. 37–72). Englewood Cliffs, NJ: Prentice-Hall, Inc.

Rudd, A. and Stoll, S. K. (1998) Understanding sportsmanship. *Journal of Physical Education, Recreation and Dance*, 69(9), 38–42.

Sage, G. H. (1986) The effects of physical activity on the social development of children. In G. H. Stull and H. M. Eckert (eds), *Effects of physical activity on children*. (pp. 22–29). Champaigne, IL: Human Kinetics.

Sage, G. H. (1990) *Power and ideology in American sport: A critical perspective*. Champaigne, IL: Human Kinetics.

Sallis, J. F. and Patrick, K. (1994) Physical activity guidelines for adolescents: Consensus statement. *British Journal of Physical Education, Research Supplement*, 15, 2–7.

Scott, G. and West. A. (1990) Pupils' attitudes towards physical education. *British Journal of Physical Education*, 21(2), 313–314.

Sharpe, T. L., Brown, M. and Crider, K. (1995) The effects of a sportsmanship curriculum intervention on generalized positive social behavior of urban elementary school students. *Journal of Applied Behavior Analysis*, 28(4), 401–416.

Sherrill, C., Holquin, O. and Caywood, A. J. (1989) Fitness, attitude towards physical education, and self-concept of elemantary school children. *Perceptual and Motor Skills*, 69(2), 411–414.

Siedentop, D. (1976) *Physical education introductory analysis*. Dubuque, IA: Wm C. Brown Company Publishers.

Siedentop, D. (1991) *Developing teaching skills in physical education*. Mountain View, CA: Mayfield Publishing Company.

Siedentop, D. (1994) *Sport education: Quality PE through positive sport experience.* Champaigne, IL: Human Kinetics.

Siedentop, D., Tousignant, M. and Parker, M. (1982) Academic learning time – physical education: 1982 revision coding manual. Unpublished manual, School of Health, Physical Education and Recreation, The Ohio State University, Columbus.

Sikes, P. J. (1988) Growing old gracefully? Age, identity and physical education. In J. Evans (ed.), *Teachers, teaching and control in physical education.* (pp. 21–40). London: Falmer Press.

Sleap, M. and Warburton, P. (1994) Physical activity levels of preadolescent children in England. *British Journal of Physical Education, Research Supplement,* 14, 2–6.

Smith, M. D., Kerr, I. G., and Meek, G. A. (1993) Physical education teacher behaviour intervention: Increasing levels of performance and motivational feedback through the utilisation of clinical supervision techniques. *Physical Education Review,* 16(2), 162–172.

Smith, M. D., Kerr, I. G. and Wang, M. Q. (1993) British physical education teacher behaviours: A descriptive-analytic study. *British Journal of Physical Education, Research Supplement,* 13, 15–21.

Smoll, F. L. and Schutz, R. W. (1980) Children's attitudes towards physical activity: A longitudinal analysis. *Journal of Sport Psychology,* 2, 137–147.

Sparkes, A. (1987) Strategic rhetoric: A constraint in changing the practice of teachers. *British Journal of Sociology of Education,* 8(1), 37–54.

Spencer, D. (1994a) No winners in PE order. *Times Educational Supplement.* November 18, 9.

Spencer, D. (1994b) Team talk for key players. *Times Educational Supplement.* December 2, 8.

Sports Council and Health Education Authority. (1992) *Allied Dunbar national fitness survey.* London: Sports Council and Health Education Authority.

Stewart, M. J. and Green, R. S. (1987) Parental attitudes toward physical education. *Physical Educator,* 44(3), 344–348.

Stiehl, J. (1993) Becoming responsible: Theoretical and practical implications. *Journal of Physical Education, Recreation and Dance,* 64(5), 38–71.

Swanson, R. A. and Spears, B. (1995) *History of sport and physical education in the United States.* Madison, WI: WCB Brown and Benchmark. (4th edition).

Talbot, M. (1993) A gendered physical education: Equality and sexism. In J. Evans (ed.), *Equality, education and physical education.* (pp. 74–89). London: Falmer.

Talbot, M. (1996) Gender and National Curriculum PE. *British Journal of Physical Education,* 27(1), 5–7.

Teacher Training Agency. (1997) *Career entry profile for newly qualified teachers.* London: Teacher Training Agency.

Templin, T. J. and Schemmp, P. G. (eds) (1989) *Socialization into physical education: Learning to teach.* Indianapolis, IN: Benchmark Press, Inc.

Tinning, R. and Siedentop, D. (1985) The characteristics of tasks and accountability in student teaching. *Journal of Teaching in Physical Education,* 4(4), 286–299.

Tousignant, M. (1981) A qualitative analysis of task structures in required physical education. Unpublished doctoral dissertation, The Ohio State University, Columbus.

Tousignant, M. and Siedentop, D. (1983) A qualitative analysis of task structures in required secondary physical education classes. *Journal of Teaching in Physical Education*, 3(1), 47–57.

Underwood, G. (1983) *The physical education curriculum in the secondary school: Planning and implementation*. London: Falmer Press.

Underwood, G. (1988) *Teaching and learning in physical education: A social psychological perspective*. London: Falmer Press.

Van Dalen, D. B. and Bennett, B. L. (1971) *A world history of physical education: Cultural, philosophical, comparative*. Englewood Cliffs, NJ: Prentice-Hall, Inc. (2nd edition).

Wang, B. M. (1977) An ethnography of a physical education class: An experiment in integrated living. Unpublished doctoral dissertation, University of North Carolina, Greensboro.

Whelan, J. (1998) Specialist sports colleges: The picture so far. *British Journal of Physical Education*, 29(3), 25–27.

Willgoose, C. E. (1984) *The curriculum in physical education*. Englewood Cliffs, NJ: Prentice-Hall, Inc.

Williams, A. (1989) Equal opportunities and primary school physical education. *British Journal of Physical Education*, 20(4), 177–179.

Index